W9-BUO-013

Reading *Adventures in Saying Yes* is so much fun you don't realize at first how profound it is. But you know you've been transformed when your first response to an unexpected and slightly frightening opportunity is, *Hmm . . . I bet Carl would say yes to this. Maybe I should say yes!* In an era when people, races, religions, and countries are being torn apart by fear, this call to move past fear and follow Jesus into caring connections is essential reading.

—**Lynne Hybels,** Advocate for Global Engagement,
Willow Creek Community Church

You'll cry. You'll laugh. You'll shake your head in disbelief. But most of all, you'll never be the same after this book. It will inspire and ignite you to go beyond planning and start prophesying your way forward in life by saying yes to Jesus' nonstop invitations to join him in what he's already up to in the world.

—**Leonard Sweet,** bestselling author, professor
(Drew University, George Fox University, Tabor College),
and chief contributor to sermons.com

We are all looking for ways to be inspired and challenged in our life with Jesus. Carl's stories don't just entertain you (even though they will). They call you to live courageously in the face of your fears.

—**Jay Pathak,** Senior Pastor, Mile High Vineyard Church,
and coauthor of *The Art of Neighboring*

Daring to go where no man has gone before, not in theory but in life itself, Carl Medearis gives us a rare look into the utterly vulnerable, harrowing, massively uplifting, and often witty adventures of one who has dared to say yes in the face of fear for the sake of the good news. What's most amazing about this book is that it all actually happened. It is said the shortest distance between truth and the human heart is story, and this is what Carl gives us: true, transparent story that leads us to unmistakable truth. Brilliant. Simply brilliant.

—**Ted Dekker,** *New York Times* bestselling author

The gospel of Jesus is not about security and segregation. It's about risk and hospitality. This is what Carl Medearis learned while living in Lebanon and shares in his thrilling book. *Adventures in Saying Yes* is a compelling call to embody the risky faith and radical hospitality of Jesus!

—**Brian Zahnd,** Pastor of Word, Life Church (St. Joseph, MO),
and author of *A Farewell to Mars*

For anyone who has ever given his or her life to follow Jesus, this book is a must read. It will press you toward a closer walk, a deeper love, and an undaunted life of following Jesus. Carl's writing is plain fun. He has a way of disarming the reader with his warm and engaging style, yet delivers deep biblical truth about what it means to be a fearless disciple. As a Lebanese immigrant to the States, I can promise you that Carl clearly understands the Lebanese culture and made me yearn for home. I was deeply moved by what God will do through us when we simply say yes.

—**Lina AbuJamra, MD,** pediatric ER doctor
and author of *Stripped: When God's Call
Turns From "Yes" to "Why Me?"*

Even if you don't like biographical books by missionaries, you are going to love this one. It's so much more than the story of a family learning how to live gracefully among Muslims. This is a text on overcoming fear, learning how to trust strangers, and allowing God to guide all you do.

—**Tony Campolo, PhD,** Eastern University

Each chapter blends extraordinary stories with those that you can easily relate to as Carl shares his adventures in working through fear and moving towards love. You'll finish this book feeling like you've made a new friend who has inspired you to take your next step toward Jesus.

—**Bruxy Cavey,** Teaching Pastor, The Meeting House

Written with real-life integrity and humor, this story explodes with invitations—to risk, to trust, to imagine, to open, to more . . .

—**Wm. Paul Young,** author of *The Shack* and *Cross Roads*

ADVENTURES IN SAYING

YES

Books by Carl Medearis

FROM BETHANY HOUSE PUBLISHERS

Adventures in Saying Yes
Muslims, Christians, and Jesus

ADVENTURES IN SAYING

YES

A JOURNEY FROM FEAR TO FAITH

CARL MEDEARIS
WITH CHRIS MEDEARIS

BETHANY HOUSE PUBLISHERS
a division of Baker Publishing Group
Minneapolis, Minnesota

© 2015 by Carl Medearis

Published by Bethany House Publishers
11400 Hampshire Avenue South
Bloomington, Minnesota 55438
www.bethanyhouse.com

Bethany House Publishers is a division of
Baker Publishing Group, Grand Rapids, Michigan

Printed in the United States of America

Library of Congress Cataloging-in-Publication Data is on file at the Library of Congress, Washington, DC.

ISBN 978-0-7642-1285-7 (pbk.)

Scripture quotations are from the Holy Bible, New International Version®. NIV®. Copyright © 1973, 1978, 1984, 2011 by Biblica, Inc.™ Used by permission of Zondervan. All rights reserved worldwide. www.zondervan.com

Some names and identifying details have been changed to protect the privacy of those involved.

Cover design by LOOK Design Studio

15   16   17   18   19   20   21   7   6   5   4   3   2   1

This one is for my family.

Not really even "for" them, as it's their story as much as mine. They lived this book and even helped write it. It's for and to and with them! The best and most wonderful wife and kids a man could ever dream of. I'm truly blessed.

I am inwardly fashioned for faith, not for fear. Fear is not my native land; faith is. I am so made that worry and anxiety are sand in the machinery of life; faith is the oil. I live better by faith and confidence than by fear, doubt, and anxiety. In anxiety and worry, my being is gasping for breath—these are not my native air. But in faith and confidence, I breathe freely—these are my native air. A Johns Hopkins University doctor says, "We do not know why it is that worriers die sooner than the non-worriers, but that is a fact." But I, who am simple of mind, think I know. We are inwardly constructed in nerve and tissue, brain cell and soul, for faith and not for fear. God made us that way. To live by worry is to live against reality.

E. Stanley Jones

Contents

Contents

Introduction

This is a book about the journey of a family. It's about war and danger and a rocky marriage and poor parenting. It's about God's grace and the Middle East and the United States and what it means to follow Jesus anywhere anytime for any reason—to jump first and ask questions later, saying yes to Jesus.

Our family is an average American family. By "average" I mean, we grew up in Beirut. There are five of us: my wife, Chris, and our three children, Anna, Marie, and Jon. Jon was born in Damascus because there was no U.S. embassy in Beirut to give him a birth certificate. Imagine—just twenty years ago it was safer in Syria than in Lebanon.

We moved to Beirut in 1992 as Christian missionaries sent out by our church and a mission organization—both great groups of people with wonderful hearts for Jesus. Our girls were babies in a double-wide stroller. Jon was born two years later. We spoke no Arabic and didn't know a single soul. Chris and I were both thirty years old and full of zeal—and a good deal of stupidity, especially me. (Patience; we'll get to that.)

You'll hear from Chris and all three of our kids, who are now young adults. We started this journey many years ago and are still living the adventure today.

That's what this book is about, a journey. With plenty of fear and a little faith.

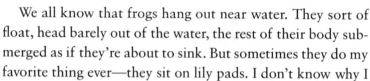

We all know that frogs hang out near water. They sort of float, head barely out of the water, the rest of their body submerged as if they're about to sink. But sometimes they do my favorite thing ever—they sit on lily pads. I don't know why I like that so much. Maybe it reminds me of some childhood book or a memory in my backyard. I'm really not sure. But I just like the thought of frogs on lily pads.

They sit there for hours. I know because I've watched for hours. I'm not sure if this is good science, but I wonder if they are afraid to jump off. Maybe they feel safe on their little green island. They can see their surroundings. Watch for the animal whose mouth is even bigger than theirs—the bass, whose main goal each day is to swallow as many frogs whole as possible.

I don't think I can prove that frogs deal with fear. I've never met a frog psychologist, but if frogs were afraid, then staying on the lily pad might be a good strategy. They blend in. They can see in all directions because they're above the water. They can catch insects without exerting much energy (a flick of the tongue, and the fly is lunch). And they can stay warm in the sun. But mostly (I'm admittedly guessing here), a lily pad provides security.

Remember Maslow's hierarchy of needs? Just above our basic need for food and water and such—foundational to all life—is safety. We need to be safe. Frogs. Humans.

We have our lily pads too. Our home is our castle. My wife prefers the King Soopers grocery store down the road to the left of our house; I prefer the one to the right. They are both exactly a half mile from our house in either direction, but I like the one, and she prefers the other. Who knows why? Maybe it's the security of familiar surroundings. In "mine," I know exactly where the cookies-and-cream ice cream is.

Feeling safe and secure is a good thing—until you don't. Stop for a moment and think of all the things that your need for security might actually stop you from doing. I can think of several. It would have stopped us from moving to Beirut, Lebanon, with two baby girls and no money, months after American hostages had been released at the end of a bloody civil war that killed 150,000 and displaced most of a nation. That thought doesn't conjure up the feeling of a snuggly warm security blanket.

Here's an easier one. Have you ever felt the urge to invite all your neighbors over for a backyard barbecue—but didn't? Why not? Maybe you realized that such a move could threaten your sense of safety and security. After all, your home is *your* castle—not theirs. What if they do weird things or ask awkward questions? Or they won't leave? Maybe they'd just all say no to your invitation, which would make you feel like you're a loser. So you don't invite them.

Or maybe your need to feel safe and secure (generally a good thing) keeps you from dreaming. You dreamt once, but it didn't work out. You even tried pursuing some big, fun exciting things another time or two, but one dream ended up costing way too much money, and the other, well, let's just say it didn't pan out. So you're done with that dreaming thing. Anyway, dreams are for dreamers. You're far too practical. You have a Larry the Cable Guy "git-r-done" mentality.

So here's my definition of fear—which is what this book is about: Fear is anything that potentially threatens your sense of safety and security.

Notice this: Fear can be based on reality, and at certain times it is a very helpful and, I'd say, God-given response. If your kitchen oven explodes in a ball of flames when you're baking your favorite blueberry pie and then immediately engulfs the rest of the room in a raging fire, it's normal to feel the slightest twinge of fear—and *run*! That's a healthy response. That kind of fear is good.

But let's be honest. How many of us have had that sort of thing happen? Most of our fears are "potential fears." What ifs. Yeah, buts. Maybes, and then whats. They're not real. They *could* be real, but they're not.

Those sorts of fears are dream squashers. They're not fun. They rob your joy. They set you back and make you grumpy.

That kind of fear keeps you from selling everything and moving to Lebanon with your young family. It keeps you firmly in the grip of words like *responsible* and the often-used *wise*. But Mr. Wisely Responsible never had much fun. He doesn't go on Hobbit-like adventures. He might save money. And he might raise three very responsible and wise children who are very well behaved. But he doesn't dream, never lives outside the box. He doesn't even know he's in a box. To him, life appears quite normal.

But I say, Leap! Dream. Say yes! Set out on an adventure—a risky journey with an uncertain outcome. Be done with being normal.

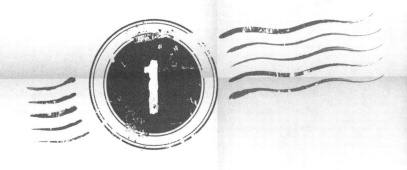

Fear Is Scary!

It is not the critic who counts. . . . The credit belongs to the man who is actually in the arena; whose face is marred by dust and sweat and blood; who strives valiantly . . . who knows the great enthusiasms . . . and spends himself in a worthy cause; who at best knows the triumph of high achievement; and who at worst, if he fails, at least fails while daring greatly, so that his place shall never be with those cold and timid souls who know neither victory nor defeat.

Theodore Roosevelt

I eagerly expect and hope that I will in no way be ashamed, but will have sufficient courage so that now as always Christ will be exalted in my body, whether by life or by death.

The apostle Paul to the Philippians

A few months ago, I got a slightly mysterious message from someone in Egypt who was supposedly the ambassador to Palestine from the Arab League. I had never heard of him and couldn't find out any information about him. Then I started getting messages from his assistant saying the Iraqi government wanted to pay for my attendance at the annual Arab League meeting on the Palestinian-Israeli issue—in Baghdad.

The way I decide such things is simple—I talk to my wife, pray, and talk to my leadership team. If no one raises any red flags, I just say yes! And that's what I did for this meeting.

That began a long back-and-forth email string about the meeting's purpose and what I would be doing. Would I be speaking? Why had they invited me? The obvious questions. But no answers. Finally, someone from Iraq's foreign ministry department said I should "submit a paper." "What kind of paper and on what topic?" I asked. No answer.

So I decided to write a paper that I'd want to present to several hundred key Arab leaders—something on Jesus (obviously). It developed into a three-page paper called "The Answer to Injustice According to Jesus of Nazareth." Basically, I wrote that the way forward depended on both divine and human forgiveness. Very controversial in such a setting, but somehow they okayed my paper.

Then I asked if I could bring some friends. "Sure," they said. I asked if my friends would get their way paid as well. "No problem," was the immediate reply. So I invited three guys crazy enough to go with me.

Three days before we were supposed to leave, the plane tickets came. Oh, and the visas had arrived the day before. We headed out—an adventure in saying yes if there ever was one.

On the way, I got a text message asking if I would "chair" one of the meetings. I had no idea what that meant—I still didn't even know what we were doing—but I said yes. We got there, and then the ambassador asked if I'd be the chairperson for two of the six main meetings. I said . . . (I think you get the idea).

It was a meeting full of Arab politicians, Palestinians, Western activists, and an interesting mix of journalists, foreign ambassadors, and even heads of state. I was put in charge of leading and moderating two of the meetings. Tell me God doesn't have a keen sense of humor. (During one of them, I wore my slippers because my feet were hurting.)

The first night, I closed with a little talk (five minutes) on prayer. I simply suggested that we needed to pray for the people of the region. You would have thought I had called for the end of the world or something. The Muslim Arabs were all elated, but the majority of the Westerners were furious. I mean, spit-coming-out-of-their-mouths angry! One woman told me, "I'm an atheist, and I can't believe you brought God into this conversation." I couldn't resist saying two things to that. First, I didn't bring God into it—he was already there and everywhere. Second, if she was an atheist, I guess she didn't need to worry, since there's no God anyway!

The next day, something similar happened when I closed by sharing my thoughts on Jesus' way—the way of forgiveness. I spoke softly and sensitively but very clearly about Jesus. I was told that had never happened before at an Arab League meeting. "Why not?" I asked. They weren't sure.

One group of Europeans actually got up and walked out. Three mothers from Gaza came up in tears. Two had lost their children, killed by Israeli shelling. They grabbed my hand and wouldn't let go. "Thank you, thank you, thank you," they repeated over and over. "Finally, someone acknowledges there is a God." The ironies here are many and profound.

The rest of the conference was full of discussions with leaders about Jesus and why I brought him into the conversation and what it meant for them now. Some incredible conversations. Too many to tell—and they continue!

It's hard to measure the success of such an endeavor. It was emotionally and physically exhausting, to be sure. I didn't give an altar call. No one "signed up" to follow Jesus. But many heard the good news that God loves and cares for them, and that Jesus' way is the way open for all. They just need to say yes.

This is pretty much how our family operates. We say yes to God and then work out the details later. Is that a smart, rational way to approach life? Maybe not. But maybe there's no such thing as a rational way to approach life. After all, a whole lot of people make decisions based on fear, and most fear is irrational.

If someone has a gun to your head and says they are going to pull the trigger—well, okay, go ahead, be afraid. That's normal. God gives us the emotion called fear to protect us. But when does normal, healthy fear turn into worry?

Worry is when we think something might happen. It is possible that if I travel to the Middle East I'll be kidnapped—so I'm not going. (And, of course, it is possible.) It is possible that if I sell everything, I'll be poor and miserable. (And that is also possible. On the other hand, you can be rich and miserable just as easily.) In other words, worry is based on worst-case scenarios. We think about how awful it would be if everything that could go wrong happened. But more often than not, the worst case doesn't happen.

I stood up to preach in a mosque packed with Shi'ite Muslims in South Lebanon and . . .

Okay, so a little context might be helpful. I'll tell you the first part of the story at the end of this book, but to jump into the middle . . . I'd been speaking about Jesus in a tent for four nights in South Lebanon—in the Hezbollah-controlled Shi'ite part. Some figured it was an amazing thing God was doing, others thought it was stupid, and I, well, I was just taking it one step at a time. We were invited back. I said yes.

We had been so well received the first time that I decided to bring my wife and two young girls down with us (Jonathan wasn't born yet).

We set up the tent and lined the ground inside with rows of white plastic chairs, a hundred in all. Before the service, about ten of us were sitting outside in a little circle, having a prayer meeting. You know the kind. Serious, but sort of perfunctory. Prayers that start with "Dear heavenly Father" and end appropriately with "in Jesus' name, amen." King James English, folded hands, bowed heads, eyes closed. You know—praying.

Suddenly two black Mercedes-Benz cars spun around the corner and nearly slid into the tent. Tinted windshields barely revealed a bunch of men in each car. It seemed like fifty guys piled out, but it might have been six. All of a sudden my mind wasn't working well, and my senses were overwhelmed with a sense of, well, something was up, and it didn't seem good.

The guys had guns. AK-47s or some other kind of Kalashnikov rifle. One man, evidently the leader, had a pistol shoved in his jeans under his belt. He was the one who yelled, "Where's the American?"

There were several nationalities in our little band of brothers, but the only Americans were my family and I—and I doubt our visitors were asking for Chris or our girls. Anyway, as I remembered it, everyone pointed to me!

I stood up, and in a second the man with the pistol was six inches from my nose, yelling, "You have to leave now, or else." When he said "or else," he made a slicing motion with his finger across his neck. I think that's a fairly universal sign—I got it. He went on to say that his sheikh (the main imam from a rival mosque in town) wasn't happy we were there, and we had to leave or something very bad would happen.

I have no idea what came over me, but I responded, "Does your imam obey God?"

Mr. Pistol in the Pants Man didn't like that question. I still remember the veins bulging from his neck as he screamed, "Of course he obeys God; he's an imam!"

"Well, I'm sort of like an imam," I said, "and I thought God had told us to come here and share Jesus with your people. But now I'm confused because your imam says not to. So, if you wouldn't mind asking him what I should do—obey God, or him?"

Honestly, I promise you, I have no idea where that came from. I wasn't feeling brave and courageous. I didn't think it through. There was no strategy to it. I had never said words like that before. Probably wasn't very smart, and I'm not sure I'd do it again. But that's what came out.

The Pistol Man looked like I'd just insulted his mother. He was furious. Without speaking (well, he did grunt), he whirled around and they all got back in their Mercedes cars and sped off.

I looked back at our neat little prayer team and everyone looked exactly like Pistol Man had—in shock. Meanwhile, our two little girls were still twirling around the tent poles inside, about thirty feet away, oblivious to all the drama. My heart suddenly exploded inside my chest as I realized that I'd just called out the local imam.

Let me just say, the prayer meeting changed tone. No more proper English well-thought-out prayers. More crying out. Our prayers were suddenly desperate—real and unscripted. Funny how that changes when you think you might die later that day.

Our little band of now-fierce prayer warriors discussed our options. It seemed that the wise and logical thing was to pack up and head home to Beirut. As we were discussing how we should do that, I leaned over and grabbed my Bible from the stool next to me. Now hear me carefully—Bible bingo doesn't usually work. When you *try* to get a verse for your situation by opening the pages randomly and reading, you'll probably turn to "And Judas hung himself," or something like that. But I was just grabbing my Bible. I wasn't thinking anything—which you'll see might be a sub-theme of this book—and my Bible opened to Isaiah 8. My eyes fell on these words in verses 11–13:

> This is what the Lord says to me with his strong hand
>   upon me, warning me not to follow the way of
>   this people:
>
> "Do not call conspiracy
>   everything this people calls a conspiracy;
> do not fear what they fear,
>   and do not dread it.
> The Lord Almighty is the one you are to regard
>   as holy,
>   he is the one you are to fear."

Did I mention that while we were praying the loudspeakers from the local mosque were blaring to the whole city: "Do not go to the tent tonight; something bad will happen. They are people who are in conspiracy with Israel. They are spies. And they drink blood." (Not sure where that last one came from—maybe because of Communion?)

Now back up a bit, and read those verses from Isaiah again.

You wanna know my immediate reaction? Honestly? I didn't want to read those verses out loud. I mean—look at them! *Do not follow the way of these people. Do not call conspiracy what they do. Do not fear what they fear. Only fear God!* Wow! I just hit the jackpot with Bible bingo—or maybe a death sentence.

24

I read the verses out loud to the whole group.

More tears.

A little confusion and more prayer.

We decided to stay. Actually, Chris and the kids went home, and a few of us guys stayed. I don't remember exactly why, but I think we wanted our little darlings out of harm's way.

The tent was packed later that night. I think the people wanted to see us drink blood. I have no idea why, but it was standing room only. I spoke from the Gospels again about God's great love for us in Christ.

At the end of the meeting, guess who showed up? Yep, Mr. Pistol in the Pants Man. He had a silly smile on his face as he shook my hand and said, "The imam liked your question, and he wants to meet you tomorrow."

What?

Sure enough, the next morning around ten o'clock, we met at the tent. The imam came with his entourage. I came with mine. He wouldn't shake my hand, which was uncharacteristic for an imam. And then he lectured me for an hour and got up to leave. As he spun around for an odd rapid exit, I asked, "Wait, sir. Can I tell you why we're here in your town? Do you even know? Do you care?"

Clearly annoyed, he said, "Hurry up. Tell me whatever you want to say."

I explained that I was from Colorado. I asked if he'd ever heard of the Rocky Mountains. He had. "Well, that's where I'm from—me and my wife and two little girls. We moved from there—sold everything—and came here. We moved to Beirut, where we live now, and then heard that some in your city wanted to know more about Jesus—how great he is and his love for your people. So we've come here. Just for that—to remind you of what I'm sure you already know: that God loves you very much and that he sent Jesus just for you."

He sat down.

We talked for another hour about Jesus. This time when he stood to leave, he extended his hand toward mine. With a firm grip, he announced, "Mr. Carl, I like you and your people. You are welcome in my city any time."

And we stayed.

This is the adventure of saying yes to Jesus!

Saying Yes to Jesus May Look Different Than You Think

I think a hero is an ordinary individual who finds the strength to persevere and endure in spite of overwhelming obstacles.

Christopher Reeve

When they saw the courage of Peter and John and realized that they were unschooled, ordinary men, they were astonished and they took note that these men had been with Jesus.

Luke, writing in Acts

Remember 1984? Not George Orwell's *1984*, but the actual year. Chris and I met that year. We were both twenty-three. Chris was the responsible one—imagine that—already teaching elementary school after graduating from Taylor University the year before. I, well, let's just say I had taken a different route after high school.

I worked a few years in construction—made a ton of money, which somehow all disappeared—and then went off with Youth With A Mission (YWAM) for ten months in Europe and the Middle East.

Three of those months I spent in a tent in a Yemen village about one hundred miles south of the capital city of Sanaa. I knew no Arabic, and no one I met knew any English. It's amazing what you can communicate through hand gestures when you have to. I was sick much of the time and got hepatitis, which put me down for about a month. I was supposed to join a whole team, but in classic YWAM style, things changed. It was mostly me and a village full of Yemenis. Countrywide, we had the brilliant idea of building outdoor bathrooms—latrines—fully equipped with nice doors, a roof, walls of plywood, and holes in the floor that allowed for a "drop" of about ten feet—dug out with rented backhoes. I even painted the outside of these beautiful houses.

The only problem was that no one wanted to "go" inside. Why go in a stinky box when the whole world is your toilet? So within a week, all the outhouses we'd built around the country were torn down, and the material was used to build extra rooms on houses. Ugh. "When Helping Hurts" lesson #1.

One day I remember men running out of my village, brandishing their AK-47s. Some jumped into the back of their shared Toyota pickup as they flew over the horizon, shouting something in Arabic. It all felt very scary and dark to me. I was sure someone would die. The twenty or so men came back a couple of hours later, chanting and cheering something. I somehow managed over the next couple of days to piece together what had happened.

A man from a nearby village had stolen something from "my" village, and the guys had gone to get it back at any cost. There had been lots of shouting and posturing and threatening, but in the end, they all drank tea together, chewed some qat—a tobacco-like stimulant—and exchanged stories of the good old days. Welcome to Arab Diplomacy 101.

I loved that place.

We can either allow ourselves to get stuck in our own rigid expectations—the way we think everything should go—or we can ask and look for the greater good. Sometimes the greater good comes in a cauldron of disappointment.

Possibly the single moment that shaped me most during that time was my brief stay at the Jibla Baptist Hospital in Yemen. One of the founding doctors and his wife had been there twenty-two years, and they were having their retirement party. Being the twenty-year-old that I was, I pressed in to ask a question.

"Dr. Yance, how many Yemenis have you seen come to the Lord?"

With such a sweet spirit, he leaned toward his wife and pondered for a full fifteen or twenty seconds before answering. "Well, son, I think maybe two. Actually depends how you count—two or three."

I was shattered. They had seen three people at the most come to know Jesus during their twenty-plus years of serving full time in Yemen at the best hospital in the country? Were they serious?

The next day, I was walking in the mountains outside my village and praying. Well, not exactly praying per se. More like yelling. Crying-yelling. I was angry at God. *How could this be?* I remember telling him, "I will *not* come out to the Middle East and give twenty-two years of my life and see two or three Muslims come to know you. I will not." (I'm not saying that this prayer was right, technically speaking, but it was, in fact, what was in my heart to say to God. And I'm pretty sure he already knew this. I think he appreciates it when we're honest about what he already knows.)

My problem was that I confused saying yes to Jesus with being overly busy and getting results. Busyness was godliness. I grew up in an environment where hard work was valued over all things—which is not all bad, of course. But when a good

WASP (White Anglo-Saxon Protestant), slightly Calvinistic work ethic combines with a bit of a messiah complex, that's a road to destruction. Add in a dose of Arminian theology that led me to believe that the faith of others depended on my preaching—well, that's just scary. In fact, I can remember my otherwise wonderful and godly grandma saying to me when I was about twelve that if someone died and they didn't know Jesus—and I hadn't preached to them—then their blood was on my head. That's a big load for a twelve-year-old to bear. And I carried that with me to Beirut.

So for me, in some healthy and unhealthy ways, landing in Beirut in the summer of 1992 was the culmination of a lifelong dream—a calling. There I was. Finally. In all humility, I could say I was God's man for the hour. Now, God didn't know that—but I was pretty sure of it. There were four million Lebanese and 250 million Arabs, and most of them didn't know Jesus—but never mind that, I was there.

Okay, so that's a slight exaggeration, but unfortunately, only a slight one. I was proud. Cocky. And stupid. A bad combination!

The first couple of months in Lebanon were glamorous, new, and exciting for Chris and me. That's how it usually is in a new country. It's called the honeymoon phase. The sounds and smells and food are all oh-so-wonderful. Everyone seemed to love us, and we loved them all in return. The Lebanese may have been the most beautiful, warm, interesting, and smart people in all the world. How did we not know this before?

And, oh my, I think everyone wanted to learn about Jesus. We could pass out tracts and Bibles on the streets, and they all wanted them. We could show the *Jesus* film, have an open-air concert, talk to our neighbors, even interact with Syrian soldiers. Everyone needed and wanted Jesus, it seemed.

31

I started a Sunday evening meeting at a local school and had over a hundred people come the first night. We soon discovered an unreached people group right under our noses—the local labor force of mostly Africans, Filipinos, and Sri Lankans. They had no church and no community. So we started one for them, and it grew like crazy. Two to three hundred were showing up every Sunday, so we started a church for them—which almost immediately became two churches. *Wow, church multiplication gone wild.* (Little did we know that the "multiplication" was due to the fact that Nigerians and Ghanaians didn't want to worship together, so they split before the church ever started. But never mind that part.) It was going great. And I was "apostle Carl" to these wonderfully open and needy people.

The local charismatic Catholic movement wanted me to train their leaders in how to run small groups. How could I say no to that?

The Lebanese evangelical churches asked me to speak somewhere almost every Sunday. Baptist and Assemblies of God, Christian and Missionary Alliance and nondenominational. Even a conservative Brethren church asked me to preach. Chris and I spent most of our time at the local Church of God (Anderson, Indiana, version), partially because its pastor was the one who provided our visas.

The Bible Society asked if I'd help give a Bible to every home. "Of course I will," I replied. Who wouldn't do that?

A large local evangelistic ministry asked if I'd be part of the leadership team and raise up the next generation of Arabs to reach out to their neighbors. Duh! "Of course I will—that's why we came."

And our neighbors. We knew we should have them over and love them and bless them and share how wonderful this Jesus is who we were following. So we did.

And—do I even need to say it?

Not only did the honeymoon phase wear off, but the next phase came with such force it almost took us out of the race. I call it the hell phase. (Not sure what the real name is, but believe me, it was real.)

While I was winning the world for Christ and training the rest of the world to do the same, Chris was in our apartment in a foreign country with little to no water or electricity. With two little babies (and a third one on the way). No friends. No family. And, for the most part, no husband. As you might guess, that didn't go too well.

Oh, and I almost forgot, on top of all this, I was teaching English and world history full-time at a Lebanese high school.

The funny ("funny" as in sad) thing was that I was receiving tons of attaboys and kudos from my fellow missionary friends and churches back home. They loved the activity. I was following Jesus, right? Doing God's will. It's hard on the family, but hey, this is the way of the kingdom.

Not.

This had nothing to do with the kingdom of God. More like the kingdom of Carl. I was having a blast, no doubt. I was exhausted, but oh, did it feel good to be working hard for God in his vineyard. In the Middle East. In a hard place like Beirut. I was created for that.

But I wasn't created for that. I was on an adventure, all right. But it was my adventure, not Jesus' adventure.

There is a way of Jesus that's hard and exciting and sometimes causes us to work long, hard hours. It can be an incredible sacrifice, even on marriages and children and health and finances. But when it's done in God's way, it brings life and lasting fruit, not relational pain to your family that harms rather than blesses. Yes, I was on an adventure, just not the right one.

I want to be careful here because there are some who need to know the fruit of hard work—who think following Jesus means life is going to be good and mostly easy. That focusing on their family means never missing a kid's game and having at least one date night a week. That being out of the house any night of the week is a sin, because they should always be there to tuck their kids in bed and snuggle up to their honey on the sofa, sipping tea and watching a romantic comedy.

I've recently wondered if our Christian culture hasn't shifted from a ministry-first mentality (not healthy) to a family-first mentality that can be just as dysfunctional. In the end, it's always God first. For those of us who are naturally disposed to overwork: We need to hear God speak *rest* to our hearts. And for those of you who think God has asked you to work exactly forty hours a week and give your life to your kids' activities and have a nice retirement plan—well, you need to hear something else from God.

Somehow, God broke through to me. He used good friends. He used my wife speaking the truth. And I needed to start noticing that the short-term success of all I was doing wasn't leading to much long-term fruit—the kind only Jesus can produce.

I needed those yeses I was saying to people and opportunities, thinking they were all a big yes to Jesus, to *actually* be a yes to Jesus.

Reluctant Courage

Take chances. Make mistakes. That's how you grow. Pain nourishes your courage. You have to fail in order to practice being brave.

Mary Tyler Moore

It is for freedom that Christ has set us free. Stand firm, then, and do not let yourselves be burdened again by a yoke of slavery.

The apostle Paul to the Galatians

It was one of those moments. But the problem with "moments" is you never know they're happening until after they happen. This particular story is full of moments when I could have said the big yes of faith or the no of fear, and I chose correctly—and so did those closest to me.

It was late one afternoon when there was a knock at our Beirut home's door. It was a Finnish man we'd met only once before. Both Chris and I happened to be home—a rare thing—and so we went outside to say hi to our unplanned guest, Mikko.

Mikko and his family had been living in south Lebanon for a couple of years. He had been with the United Nations, serving along the border with Israel as part of a U.N. peacekeeping force, and then he decided to bring his family and stay longer in the region to serve God there. He was known for being fearless. Maybe not the sharpest tool in the shed, but fearless nonetheless. The one other time I'd met Mikko was in the southern Lebanese city of Tyre (yep, the one from the Bible). I was there visiting a friend and noticed Mikko standing on the street corner passing out something from a big box. He was pretty easy to spot with his snowy-white skin and bleached blond hair—obviously not from around those parts. I stopped to find out who he was and what he was doing.

I walked up to him and said hi, introducing myself. He responded with something like, "I Mikko. I give Bibles." There you go. That was pretty much it. He was handing out Bibles on the streets of very-Muslim Tyre.

Now here he was at my door, and the first thing he did was point to his beat-up Land Rover with a big white bundle strapped to the roof. "I have tent," he told me.

Great. A tent.

"So what's it for?" I asked, not really sure if I even wanted to know.

"Me set tent in south; you preach."

Thus was the conversation. It lasted about ten minutes, and then Mikko drove off. I wasn't really sure what had just happened. I did know that he lived in a totally Shi'ite part of south Lebanon and that their home was often a near miss by rockets from all sides. He later joked with me, saying that they didn't need to till their garden because the bombs did it for them.

I sort of forgot our conversation until Mikko showed up at our house about a month later. He asked if I'd come to the south and meet with a friend of his. This Muslim friend wanted to know more about Jesus. Well, that was an easy one. "Of course," I said. I'm always up for such meetings.

The man Mikko wanted me to meet lived in a city called Cana, about half an hour inland from Tyre and twenty miles north of the Israeli border—100 percent Shi'ite Muslim. I'd never been there before. I found a young Lebanese friend who was brave enough to venture into Hezbollah territory with me, and we headed south.

I'll never forget the moment. We rounded a corner in the small 5,000-person town of Cana into the central open square—and there, right in the middle of the town, was a white tent and its very white owner beaming from ear to ear, waiting outside for us.

It's an interesting sidenote that the Muslim residents of Cana believe that this is the Cana where Jesus turned water into wine, and they're quite proud of the fact. There's also a Cana in northern Israel that's more likely to be the one, but who knows—Jesus was in this part of the world, so it could be.

Anyway, here I was, now standing next to Mikko and his tent, wondering what in the world was going on. "What's up with the tent, Mikko?"

Excitedly, he showed me the flyers he had passed around town earlier that day. I had my Lebanese friend read them, as I didn't (and still don't) read Arabic. Mikko had passed out five hundred flyers inviting people to come to the tent that night to hear "a man preach about Jesus."

"Really?" I asked with a mix of anger and shock—as it sank in who that preacher was. I mean, I'm a trained Christian missionary. We have faith and all that, but seriously, you don't just set up a tent in a Shi'ite city and preach Christ and hope it goes well. That'd be nonsense.

Well, that was Mikko's plan. "Oh, one thing," he added, "the Hezbollah leader wants to meet you first."

Oh, sure he does. So he can take me out—and not for dinner.

But I was curious. And the next thing I knew, before I really had time to think it through, Mikko and I were at the Shi'ite leader's home. And oh, I almost forgot—my young Lebanese "assistant," who was from a Christian background and had seen these very people in much different circumstances during the years of civil war, was about to wet his pants. In fact, I had to pull the car over so he could lean out the window and expel the contents of his stomach on the side of the narrow road leading to the regional leader's house.

We arrived to a typically warm Arab reception. Tea and cookies and initial friendly remarks about the health of our families and lots of "God willing, everyone is healthy" all in the first two minutes. Then we settled into the white plastic picnic chairs that thrive in that part of the world (man, I should have invented white plastic chairs—I'd be rich).

Near the Hezbollah leader on his front porch were two of his brothers and two other men who also seemed to be "brothers," but from another mother. They all brandished the weapon of choice—Kalishnikov assault rifles.

Five minutes and two sips of tea later, the Shi'ite said, "*Ahlan wa Sahlan.*" Basically, it means, "You are welcome here."

"*Shukran,*" I replied ("thank you," as you might guess).

He went on to say how happy he was that we were there, and if we needed anything, he'd be happy to help. I remember thinking it was at least a little odd that he seemed so happy to welcome us, given that the plan was for me to speak of Christ that night to the people of his region. "The Tent" had created quite a buzz, and Mikko was expecting a full tent. I still hadn't quite signed on with the program, but was starting to feel encouraged.

I didn't want the Hezbollah leader to be surprised later that evening, so I thought I should ask him simply what he thought would be happening in The Tent. Mikko couldn't speak Arabic, and the man obviously didn't speak Finnish—and the English of neither one was good enough for more than simple greetings, so I was wondering how he even knew what would be happening (or might be happening) that night. *Maybe he has read the flyers*, I thought to myself. *But I'd better ask—just in case . . .*

"So, do you understand what Mikko wants to do tonight?" (I was totally blaming this whole thing on Mikko at this point—no ownership just yet.)

"Oh no, but that's okay. We just want the world to know that we're not monsters and that we're happy to welcome foreigners and even Americans to our city." *Oh. My. Goodness. He doesn't know what's going on at The Tent.*

With a sideways glare at Mikko, I dove in—figured I might as well just tell him. It went like this: "Mikko had this idea to set up the tent and invite me to come and speak about Jesus tonight. And he said it was okay, and that you just wanted to talk first, but if it's not—" What a wimpy statement.

"So, if it's okay, we might want to go ahead and just talk about Jesus a little bit tonight with the people of Cana. That's if you're totally okay with it, of course." Not exactly the speech William Wallace gave in *Braveheart* before they attacked the English forces.

There was a brief pause, and the man jumped to his feet. I promise you, I thought that was it for me. The end. *Jesus, here I come*, I thought as my heart tried to exit my chest, held in only by my T-shirt. He threw his hands in the air, at which point I flinched, wondering what a bullet would feel like, or would the next thing I knew I'd be in heaven with God, or did I have to wait a bit for everyone else to join, or—

"This is great!" he shouted. "Wonderful. We need to know more about the prophet Jesus." Believe me, this was not the time to argue whether Jesus was only a prophet or something more.

"What?" I blurted back in shock.

"Yes, we're not good Muslims because we know *some* of the prophets but not all of them. And we especially need to know more about *Sayeedna Isa*" (our Lord Jesus).

"This is fantastic," he continued. "I will send my brothers here to help you out tonight." He waved his hand at the four guys next to him, who all looked about as confused as I did. The only one who didn't look confused was Mikko. He was just smiling. Of course, my young Lebanese friend was about to pass out from fear, then confusion, followed by excitement—too many life-altering emotions in the span of a few minutes for him. I actually think he blacked out in his chair for a few seconds. Seriously.

As we drove off, I realized I would be preaching about Jesus in a tent that night in a Shi'ite town in southern Lebanon—across from the United Nations' main base for that whole region. I may have forgotten to mention that part. The field where the tent was pitched was literally across the street from the U.N. Army base. Just for some added dramatic effect.

We scrambled to get ready, my head spinning. *What should I say? Should I go for it, or sort of play it safe?* I mean, no one would call what we were doing "playing it safe," so I guessed I should just tell a couple of nice Jesus stories and we'd all go home happy. Muslims are fine with Jesus. They like him quite a lot actually. Just don't talk right away about the crucifixion and resurrection, or that he's God in the flesh and the only way to a relationship with God the Father. Obviously, there's quite a lot that Muslims are not okay with, but you can talk for hours about Jesus, retelling the parables, things he taught and did, even his miracles, and they'll be delighted.

The tent was full, and I spoke from John chapter 1. I had decided not to hold back. This whole thing was so weird anyway—*might as well go for it.* I mean, it wasn't like I gave an altar call or something super crazy. I just spoke for forty-five minutes—through a translator—about how good Jesus was and is.

At the end of my talk, Mikko stood up and announced that we'd be back the next night. I don't remember discussing that, but he looked at me in front of the whole audience, and all I could do was nod my head yes.

We did that three nights in a row. Each night, Mikko surprising me with "and tomorrow night we will . . ."

At the end of the third night, he announced that we'd be showing a movie the following night. It was the *Jesus* film—though he didn't really mention that. He just said it was a movie.

The place was packed that fourth night. In fact, we took the tent down and just set up in the open field—for about three hundred Shi'ite friends. Many had truly become quick friends of ours. We'd been eating lunches and dinners in their homes and playing soccer with their kids during the days.

At the end of the *Jesus* film, we invited anyone who wanted to give their lives to following Jesus to stand up. About forty did. The whole week had been stunning. Powerful. Miraculous. Talk about an adventure.

We packed up around midnight, and my poor little Lebanese friend and I started on the three-hour drive back to Beirut. On the way home, we stopped for a quick break at the only shop still open. The region is littered with these hole-in-the-wall *dikaans*. My young friend and I walked in, got two Cokes, and decided to sit in the white plastic chairs and just breathe a moment while we sipped our sodas. We were exhausted. But it was a good tired.

As we were about to leave, a man stumbled in, dragging his left leg behind him. It honestly looked like he was pulling on a log—but it was his leg. He slouched into a white chair opposite ours, groaning in obvious pain. The looks on our faces must have begged an explanation, because he offered one: "I was working on my son's new home, which is being built on top of mine, and I fell on the rebar [steel rod] that was sticking out of our roof to connect the new concrete of his floor to ours. It poked all the way through my leg, right here under my kneecap."

I didn't really need to see that, but he opened up the slit in his pant leg and showed us something that looked more like a rotten watermelon than a knee. It was full of pus, swollen to twice its original size or more, and was going to be amputated the next day up in Beirut. My Coke almost didn't stay down.

My otherwise mute and fear-bound eighteen-year-old Lebanese Christian friend volunteered me to pray for him. *What?* My friend went into this whole deal about how Jesus heals people, to which Muhammad exuberantly agreed (yes, his name really was Muhammad—which doesn't give away much, as every fourth person is named that). In fact, Muhammad then told us a story about his cousin who was once healed from a serious disease by watching Pat Robertson on the *700 Club* once. I mean, you can't make this stuff up.

So after my Lebanese friend and I argued for a few minutes over who should pray for Muhammad—I said it should be him since it was his brilliant idea—I finally agreed to. Now, I don't know what your theology of healing is, but it's probably a lot like mine. Ready for it? That God *can* heal anyone—he just doesn't do so when you and I pray for someone. Am I right? My theology of healing also says that God heals people in regions that I've not visited—like Argentina, India, or most of Africa. I believe he can. I've heard about it. I've prayed for some headaches that seemed to get a little better. But serious stuff like healing someone's knee that looks like a war zone—nope. Never seen it. It's not that I don't believe it could happen; it's just that I don't think it's going to happen.

So I prayed one of "those" prayers—you know the type: "Dear Jesus, if it is your will (which I doubt it is), help the doctors and comfort this man's family." You know the kind we pray that covers all the bases because we're positive that nothing's going to happen anyway. I prayed possibly the wimpiest prayer in the history of praying. About thirty seconds long. I ended it with "in Jesus' name, amen" like you're supposed to, and then, as I got up to leave, told the man, "Well, it was nice to meet you, Muhammad, and I hope it goes well tomorrow in Beirut." Did I mention I was exhausted? I had come down for one day, which ended up being four, and I needed/wanted to get home to my family.

I still don't understand what happened next. Muhammad let out a yell, sort of like a war cry, and when I turned around, he was running past me out the front door. This is beyond hilarious, but just as he ran out (though I couldn't figure out how he could be running in the first place), he slammed into the side of a panel truck delivering potato chips to the little shop.

Wham! The smack sounded like a rifle shot. The driver, thinking he'd run over this guy, jumped out and said, "I'm so sorry! Are you okay?" To which Muhammad replied, "Yes, that evangelist in there prayed to Jesus and my leg is healed."

Wait now—let's slow down for a second. My heart's pounding just remembering and writing the story. I need a second . . .

First of all, "that evangelist prayed to Jesus" statement? Huh? I've never called myself an evangelist. *Where'd he get that?* It's interesting that the Arabic word for *evangelist* literally translates (like the Greek word would have) as "one who shares good news." A good-newser.

I looked at the back of Muhammad's pant leg and it was straight. Limp. Like normal.

My friend and I sat there stunned as Muhammad started recounting the whole thing to this confused panel-truck driver.

If you remember, this "evangelist" had no faith for any of this. My Lebanese friend had some. Muhammad had a lot. And somehow it worked. I mean, like, really worked. He was healed.

Just then, the shopkeeper walked up to me and, with an incredulous look, said, "Whoa—can you come upstairs and heal my son?"

I immediately launched into a theological discourse on how I wasn't "a healer" but sometimes Jesus heals (evidently) and that I'd be happy to pray for his son but maybe now was not the best time to do that since it was one in the morning and . . .

He was having none of it. I noticed neither he nor Muhammad cared one bit about my theology of healing. Odd.

The next thing I knew, we were upstairs—above the little shop where Muhammad had now gathered a small crowd as he told and retold his story. But the shop owner's son was not home. Abu Joseph—that was the shopkeeper's name—then slumped to the floor and began to cry as he recounted how he'd come to The Tent meetings that week and heard about Jesus. He began to cry out to God and repent for not being a good husband and father. In the middle of this, his wife, who had been at her sister's house, walked in. We actually had our hands on his back praying for him while he was in tears on his living room floor. She sort of freaked out because it looked like we were hurting him—him crying and two strange men with their hands on his back. And she had also just walked through a crazy crowd down below.

"What's going on around here?" she asked. Good question.

Abu Joseph explained the whole night, and it wasn't long before they were both giving their lives to Jesus. And as they were doing that, the son came in—around two o'clock. He couldn't speak or hear—since birth. Through sign language the mother and father explained the whole night to him, and we prayed for his healing. Ironically, I had some faith for that one, but he didn't get healed. So there you go—shows what I know.

By three that morning I couldn't stand up anymore. As we were leaving, Abu Joseph said, "Oh, one more thing. My other son just got back from a quick trip to Ghana where he does some work in Africa, and I know he'd want to meet you. He's very interested in Jesus and spiritual things."

I didn't know how to turn him down and still have some sense of godliness about me, but I begged him to let us go home. "I'm sure your son and his family will be sound asleep, and it'd be rude to wake them," I whined. "We live in Beirut; I'll come back next week. Really, I have to go."

So, as you've guessed by now, we found ourselves walking through our new crowd of faithful and confused friends—somehow without even being noticed by them—down a dark, narrow street to Abu Joseph's son's house. We just walked right in, with the dad yelling, "Hey, get out of bed! You need to come out here." Hassan, the son, stumbled out of his bedroom, followed by his wife, as they both closed their robes and asked what the emergency was.

Abu Joseph explained the whole night yet again.

Hassan was stunned. His first words were, "That's strange, because right before I left for Africa five days ago, I told my Finnish friend Mikko that I had to know about Jesus now, and Mikko told me he'd bring a friend down to tell me. Are you him?"

You can say no to Jesus if you want to. But this is what happens when you say yes.

It's True—Sharks Might Eat You, and the Neighbors Are Scary

We are continually faced by great opportunities brilliantly disguised as insoluble problems.

Lee Iacocca

Be strong and very courageous.

God to Joshua

Not sure if you've ever gone diving. I haven't. I've snorkeled a few times. I remember the first time well. We were on a family vacation in Sharm el Sheikh, a magical place on the southern tip of the Sinai Peninsula in Egypt. A pure holiday town—Arab style. In other words, wonderful hospitality, amazing weather, gorgeous views, a little messy, and slightly confusing.

We were going to be snorkeling in the Red Sea. I was given the mask and the tube (snorkel) that connects to the side of the mask. After jumping off the end of the pier that jutted out into the sea, I was told to get the mask good and wet, so I did. I slid it over my eyes and wiggled it until the mask suctioned onto and around my nose and eyes, and then I adjusted the snorkel so it would be sticking up into the air when I looked into the water.

I was ready to go. All I needed to do now was float on my belly and stick my head in the water. I positioned the snorkel in my mouth and stuck my head underwater. I wasn't sure what I was expecting to see—fish and coral, I suppose—but it scared the snot out of me! Literally. I choked, coughed, blew boogers all over the inside of my mask, and came thrashing up out of the water, thinking I was drowning.

Why? Because I was in shock. I had never imagined that I'd see what I saw. Colors on fish I didn't know existed. Bright, bright orange. A red color that was so bright it was scary—like an apple on fire.

I freaked out. I was surprised. Scared and confused. All from simply sticking my head into clear twenty-foot-deep Red Sea water.

So that's why I've never been diving. I can't imagine how freaky that would be. If I can't handle snorkeling, surely diving would be the end of me.

Who knows what's down there? Unimaginable things of legends. Giant squid. We've recently seen the images of them lurking in the depths of the sea, just waiting to entangle unsuspecting divers. There are things that sting, squeeze, chomp, and poke, and that are thinking about how to eat divers. Worst of all—there's the darkness. I've never been down there, but I've heard it gets so dark you can't even see the shark when it's about to turn your head into fish chum.

That's some scary stuff. And it's all true. Therefore, obviously, I don't go diving.

What's that? No, well, no, I've never experienced any of that. But I haven't experienced those horrible things because I'm not dumb enough to do it. Never mind that I don't personally know anyone who's actually had their head turned into fish food by a shark or any other of those horrible things I just described. But I know it's so because I've seen it on TV. I've heard of the jellyfish off the coast of Australia. And the giant stingray that stabbed what's-his-name who was filming a new TV show. And the surfer off the coast of somewhere—South Africa, I think—who got cut in half by a Great White. I'm not dumb. I've seen *Jaws*. This stuff is real. It happens, and it ain't happening to me! Because I'm not diving!

And honestly, never mind the details of what will happen to you if you foolishly decide to ignore my advice and dive into the depths of who knows where—just think about the darkness part of it all. Have you ever heard of anything good happening after dark? I don't think so! Why do we tell our kids to be home before dark? Why are murders and muggings and all types of horrible things always happening after dark? Because you can't see. That's why!

Why does Scripture always talk about light and dark? Light—good. Dark—bad. You know, "You were once darkness, but now you are light." Darkness breeds monsters. Scary stuff. Bad. Yucky. Freaky. Dark.

And diving deep leads to the dark—don't do it!

So how do I know about all that scary stuff? Well, the same way you "know." We've been told.

How do we "know" that if we go "over there" we're going to die? How do we "know" that traveling to the Middle East will surely mean we'll be immediately kidnapped, or worse? How do we "know" that being kind to a person with AIDS exposes us to the disease and we might catch it? How do we "know" that selling our extra cars, or our houses, or giving away all of our money will mean that we'll starve?

But switching from the theoretical (sharks) to the very practical—neighbors . . .

Ours are like yours. Some are great. A few not really bad, and some, well, how do I say it? A little odd. (By the way, our physical neighbors read my books, so I need to be careful.)

When our family moved back from Beirut, we bought a house. Now that's scary. Anyway, we did it—jumped in and became fairly common suburban homeowners. We live on a cul-de-sac, which is amazing because we can hear all of our neighbors' arguments. We have a golden retriever and even a Chevy Suburban (to round out the "suburban" feel). I know, I know, I can hear you now—"So, the ol' Carl the-amazing-Middle-Eastern-conquer-the-world guy is a suburban home-owner, eh?"

Yep, busted. I mean, all the other stuff is true and still hap-pens regularly, but yes, for the last few years we've been here in good ol' American Highlands Ranch, Colorado.

Back to the neighbors.

You'd be shocked at how intimidating they were when we first moved in. All-white American and Republican and Catho-lic. Who were these people? Give us some brown-skinned Arabs and we're good. But these folks? Oh, they seemed friendly—odd, since everyone had told us that a suburb of Denver like ours would definitely not be friendly; they were probably just faking it.

And there was this one family of three to our left that everyone very quickly told us was odd. In fact, she was from Russia. Imagine—a Russian living next to us. Probably a spy. The weird thing is, she brought us chocolate chip cook-ies the day after we moved in. Sounding like one of the Rus-sians from the movie *Spies Like Us*, she said, "*Velcome* to the *neigh-boo-hood*."

Yeah, right. We had heard about this family. Nothing spe-cific, just that they were odd and "kept to themselves." Very spooky.

But wow, those cookies were tasty.

Honestly, though, it felt a bit intimidating to be in the United States, in general, and in this neighborhood specifically. Everyone was actually quite friendly and made us feel welcome, but we weren't sure if they really wanted to be friends. And our definition of "being a friend" was now shaped by twelve years in the Arab world, where being a friend means you hang out all the time in each other's home, on the street, in cafés, and together at the beach or the mountains on the weekends for multi-family picnics with homemade hummus and baba ghanouj. We were fairly sure that wasn't what friendship meant here—but what *did* it mean? We had no idea. Garage door goes up. Car drives in. Garage door goes down. And that's it. An occasional quick rendezvous at the shared cul-de-sac mailbox, and all's good. Suburbia.

But shouldn't we believe that neighbors everywhere are hungry for deep friendship with both God and humans—just like we are? Chris and I believe that, so we formulated a plan. It wasn't very spectacular, this plan. It was sort of basic and remedial. We decided to knock on all our neighbors' doors—all on the same Tuesday evening—and ask each of them if they'd want to come to our house that Friday night and discuss doing a "Jesus study" together.

So we did. We knocked on Bob and Kylie's door. They opened and invited us in.

"Wassup?" they asked in their friendly, neighborly way.

"Well, Chris and I were just wondering—since we're all so happy to be neighbors and, I'm sure, looking for some ways to connect—if you'd want to come over this Friday night and discuss whether we'd all like to do a Jesus study. You know, it might be a good way for all of us to get to know each other more around a shared topic."

"Hmmm," Bob said, looking slightly confused. "A Jesus study, eh? What is that? Like a Christian Bible study?"

"Nope," I quickly corrected. "Not Christian and not a Bible study. Just studying the life of Jesus."

"Oh," they both replied—as if what I said really explained anything. "Sure. What time?"

A little surprised that this had taken a total of, like, three minutes since we had rung the doorbell, and not really prepared with anything that sounded like a real plan, I said, "Well, how about seven?"

"Great. We'll be there."

We chatted for a few more minutes and left for the next house.

"That wasn't so bad," Chris exclaimed with a slight sense of optimism. I just nodded my head as if I'd known that's what was going to happen. Yeah, right!

Next house—very similar conversation. We ended up visiting five neighbors that night, and they all said yes. One couple was pretty concerned that this was an evangelistic attempt to make them Christians. With total integrity, we sort of chuckled and said something like, "Oh yeah, we've done that before—doesn't work that well—so nope, this is not that. We really do just want to look at the life of Jesus." They were convinced enough to say they'd come that Friday.

But you know how that goes. People *say* they'll do stuff, but don't really mean it. But guess what? Everyone came. All the couples. We had a house full of about fourteen adults.

Long, fun story for another time. But we did it. We started, and it has been awesome.

It's funny to think back to that wonderful night several years ago when Chris and I got over ourselves and went for it. No fear. Well, okay, that's not true. We had fear. We felt totally insecure and embarrassed. What if they thought we were weird (which has been confirmed, by the way)? Or what if they just said no? Or didn't open the door when we knew they were home? Just the thoughts of those things almost made us not do it. Imagine.

But this time, fear didn't win.

"I'm a Normal Person!"
(Chris's Story)

For I was hungry and you gave me something to eat, I was thirsty and you gave me something to drink, I was a stranger and you invited me in, I needed clothes and you clothed me, I was sick and you looked after me, I was in prison and you came to visit me.

Jesus' words in Matthew

Chris

Lest you think this book was written by a cruel man who drags his unwilling family all over the world on his crazy adventures, I wanted to give you my perspective.

When Carl asked me to write a few stories about faith overcoming fear, I immediately became full of fear and thought, *What can I possibly say that people will want to hear?* I then realized that my journey in life has been quite different from Carl's, but we both have experienced God rescuing us, reviving us, reminding us, revealing to us, and reconciling us to his love, which, when glimpsed, sets us free from the fear that so easily entangles us. So, because of my gratitude to God for his tenderness toward me, I decided to share a few of the many encounters I have had with God in times of fear.

Let me begin by saying my early childhood was one of love, laughter, and a close-knit family. I am from a family of eight children. I am fourth from the oldest. My father was a doctor who emigrated from Greece in his late twenties. He ended up finishing his residency in Chicago and met my mother, who was a nurse, at a beach party on Lake Michigan. My mother's parents were from Czechoslovakia. Since my father was the more outgoing and verbal one, we ended up being more Greek in customs and culture. Life was grand.

That changed in the middle of the night one early spring, just a month and a half before I would graduate from high school. I was awakened by my father shouting, "Come quickly. Mom is not breathing!"

We all ran to the bedside, and after calling for an ambulance, my father, with tears streaming down his cheeks, tried to resuscitate her, but she was not responding. I wanted so badly for this to just be a nightmare that I would wake up from, but the ambulance arrived, and my dad and I went to the hospital where they pronounced her dead. She had died from an aneurysm at the age of forty-four.

The previous night, before we all went to bed, my mom had just returned from having coffee with a friend, and we had such a pleasant conversation. My sisters and I were sitting in their bedroom while my mom chatted about the nice time she had, and then spun off into saying how grateful and happy she was that she had had all eight of us. Those final words ring in my ears to this day.

This first traumatic experience in my life left me brokenhearted and deeply wounded. We all were so afraid that death would return that we lined up our sleeping bags in our living room and slept in one room.

On the day of her funeral, the heavens opened and rain poured down that day and for several more. It made me feel like no sufficient amount of tears could be shed in those days. We lived in a small town, and people responded with such love and concern. At the time, I was the oldest sibling still living at home. Fear and anger took root in my heart, and I kept asking

God, "Why?" I started to operate not out of a sound mind but out of fear. I became agoraphobic and had a hard time leaving the house on my own.

I did end up going to college in the fall at my father's insistence. My mom was the one who had taken me on the college visit where I applied and eventually attended. When classes began, I was excited but still fearful. I usually went home every weekend that fall because I was not very stable. I thought that by attending a Christian college, maybe I could find answers to the pain I was experiencing. Instead, my vulnerable heart would be tread upon again.

It was a weekend that I didn't go home. I was crying in my room, and my roommate walked in and asked what was wrong. I hadn't told her about my mom, but when I shared the source of my grief, she shocked me by saying something to the effect of, "Well, it's not like you lost one of your arms or legs." I retorted, "I'd give all my limbs to have my mother back." After this experience and several others, I guarded my heart and words more and started to shut down. My front tooth became discolored and my hair started to fall out. Needless to say, I was a real mess.

My older sister, a strong believer, saw the state I was in and poured out her concern for me through phone calls and letters. She signed me up for Urbana 1979, the student mission conference that was to take place at the University of Illinois over Christmas break. She never really told me what Urbana was, because she knew I would be hesitant if it was "a Christian thing," so she said it was a conference with people from all over the world coming together to express their love and concern for the world. I am so glad I decided to go. The many wonderful speakers and workshops helped my heart experience perfect love for the first time and cast out a little of the fear that bound me so. I still remember a gentleman who shared the story of the prodigal son, not through words but with artistic stick figures. He had worked in Africa sharing Jesus. That day, it was good news for me.

That January we could take a single class for a month as part of the college's J-term, but I opted out and went home. When I returned to college, a new roommate helped life look a bit brighter for me. I do not have hard feelings toward my first roommate; I have forgiven her, and I realize that some people just don't know what to say when someone is hurting. I think it is nice to simply say, "I'm sorry," and to just listen.

I made a lot of great friends over the remaining years at college, many very devoted to and full of God, which challenged me more to seek out his amazing love. I graduated from college as an elementary school teacher and landed a job in Colorado Springs at a wonderful Christian school. My heart continued to heal during that time, and I learned so much about the Bible and how it helps us navigate through life, in good times and in bad.

My first year of teaching is when I met Carl through mutual friends, and boy, did life change—for the better! I loved Carl's passion for God, his great sense of humor, and his way with people. It wasn't long before we were dreaming about marriage and where we might live and serve. Only through God's love and grace could I ever imagine dreaming like this. Remember, I was the one who had a hard time even leaving my home.

It's funny now that the first place Carl suggested we live was Beirut, Lebanon. We were just getting serious in our relationship when he asked me, "Do you feel called to Beirut?" The year was 1984, and Lebanon was in the middle of a brutal civil war marked by frequent kidnappings of foreigners.

"No!" I replied, which Carl met with, "Well, then we can't date anymore." One thing was clear to me at the time: he was quite set on this Beirut idea.

The next day, I flew to my small hometown near Chicago for summer vacation. Within twenty-four hours, Carl called.

"Uh, well, maybe it isn't time," he said.

"For us, or for Beirut?"

I could hear him swallow. "For Beirut."

Yes, I guess Carl kind of liked me. Yet I knew he was disappointed that we wouldn't be leaving anytime soon for Beirut.

But I love how God's timing is always better than our own. In 1991, Carl, our daughter Anna, who was six months old, and I took a scouting trip to Greece and Cyprus, thinking we would serve in one of those countries. But neither seemed right for us. While we were in Cyprus, though, we kept meeting so many wonderful Lebanese people who had moved there because of the war back in their country. One quiet evening, I felt like God gave me a prompting that we should go to Lebanon. When I told Carl, he was over the moon and grinned from ear to ear.

Lebanon was only a half-hour plane ride from Cyprus, but we were out of money, so instead of visiting Beirut, we just trusted that we had heard God correctly and went home and prepared for our big move. In a year's time we were able to pay off our debts and raise some support. It was a tremendous help that our good friends kindly invited us to live in their basement rent free during that period. In that year of preparation, we even expanded our family and added our precious daughter Marie. Needless to say, we were quite busy.

In our final days in the States, we had a garage sale to get rid of everything we owned. We ended up with a whopping seven hundred dollars—and four hundred dollars of that came from selling an old Dodge truck, our biggest-ticket item. Soon after, we were saying our good-byes to family and friends and flying off with our two baby daughters and four suitcases.

We first flew to Belgium and then to Greece, and then we took a boat to Cyprus. From there we got on another plane and finally touched down in Beirut. The adventure was only beginning, though. When we hit the tarmac, our plane caught on fire. Normally, I would have freaked out, but I just knew we'd be okay. I think my peace was from God—but it could have been fatigue! The Lebanese gentleman who picked us up later said, "Wow, you came in like Elijah, on chariots of fire. And today is St. Elijah's Day!"

Our drive from the airport was eerie. The streets were lined with burned-out cars among army tanks, uniformed soldiers, and tall concrete buildings pockmarked from gunfire and shellings. Some buildings were totally flattened or left half standing. There were army checkpoints all along the way, which interrupted our journey about every fifteen minutes. My eyes must have been as big as saucers as I gazed out the window at the new world we were entering. New language, new faces, new terrain, new smells, and new sounds put my whole being on overload. I desperately needed something that I could identify with or anchor to.

We arrived at the village we would be staying at and I found that our host's family name stirred memories in me. If you recall, I grew up Greek, and every Sunday our family had attended a small Greek Orthodox church. There weren't many Greeks in our town, so anyone who was Eastern Orthodox—Lebanese, Syrians, Jordanians, Palestinians—worshiped in our tiny church. I was surrounded by Khourys, Malooleys, Trahds, Maloufs, Khaleels, and Saabahs. I remember telling Carl how amazing it was that God knew those wonderful memories and family names from my childhood would comfort me one day.

Our first years in Lebanon were humbling. I missed my family and friends tremendously. I cried a lot, and was quite a wimp. I had no idea how to live in a place that still had open wounds from sixteen years of battles. We didn't have steady electricity or running water. The electricity would come and go. Sometimes we wouldn't have electricity for two weeks or more. I remember going to the landlady once and saying, "You know, we haven't had electricity for thirteen days. When do you think we will have it?" She told me, "During the war, we didn't have it for thirteen months, and we would sit in the stairwells with candles and wait for the shelling and bombing to subside." Hearing that, I crawled home and determined not to complain. We also had to wait for water trucks to come and fill the tanks perched on our rooftop. This was a sporadic event as well.

61

Another challenge was that I had no idea how to cook when we moved to Beirut, because everything had to be made from scratch. When I walked into the market, there were bags of flour, lentils, rice, vegetables, and a butcher. Not a can could be found to simply open and heat in a microwave. The first time I purchased a whole chicken, it was wrapped in a plastic bag, and when I pulled it out, it still had the head and legs and feet on it. I felt like the crazy bird was looking at me. I think I screamed, and Carl just roared with laughter. Thankfully, with help from my wonderful Lebanese neighbors, I learned to cook quite delicious food, though never as good as theirs. They were so amazingly patient with me, and I think I blessed them with laughter.

Carl and I did not have a lot of money in those early days. A big treat was going out for a rotisserie chicken and French fries. The best part was the garlic sauce you could dip your fries in or put on the chicken. The kids loved this garlic sauce, too. It was so strong that even after they brushed their teeth, they smelled of garlic when we kissed them good night. Sometimes our funds ran low, and we didn't have much money for groceries. One night the girls were crying because they were hungry. Carl was gone that evening, and I felt like crying, too. A loud knock on the door surprised me, and an elderly Lebanese lady who lived down a little rocky road from our house was standing there with a huge tray of food. She said to me in English, "I thought maybe you needed this." Tears came to my eyes, but from gratitude. I thanked her and invited her in, but she quietly went on her way. I felt like I had been visited by an angel. Food never tasted so delicious.

When I think of Jesus' words in Matthew 25:35–36 (quoted at the beginning of this chapter), I think of all the Lebanese neighbors and friends who responded to us with such love, kindness, and warm hospitality. I am forever indebted to them. We have countless stories of meals around Lebanese tables lavished with delicious foods stretching from one end of the table to the other. The conversations were usually deep and meaningful.

They welcomed us in as strangers, and we said our good-byes at the door as friends.

Sometimes when the kids and I would be out for a stroll, a woman would say, "Come and drink coffee," and motion me into her home. The Lebanese love children, and they would often bring out a tray of juice and little cookies, all served with a smile. Another wonderful memory from those frequent visits was how they would pick up a piece of fruit—whatever was in season—and start peeling it and slicing it up and then serving it to you. Hospitality in Lebanon was like medicine for a weary, lonely, burdened soul.

The verse in Matthew 25 about needing clothes hit home for me during this time, but with a twist. My long denim skirts apparently made me look like I was from the 1800s, straight out of the TV series *Little House on the Prairie*. One day an upstairs neighbor bluntly asked me, "Do you have any other clothes?" I wasn't sure why she was so concerned, but she took me shopping and helped me jazz up my wardrobe a bit. The Lebanese are beautiful people, and I can tell you, they dress to the nines. I never really did catch up to their fashion standards, but they still loved and accepted me.

When any of us were sick, friends were quick to visit and bring us soup or special herbs. When the children needed to see a doctor, my Lebanese friends would go with me until they felt I could navigate on my own.

In Matthew 25:36, Jesus talks about prison. I was never in prison physically, but isn't it true that when we allow fear, loneliness, or heartache to overcome us, we build walls that imprison us? During my sad and lonely times, neighbors inevitably knew to come over and cheer me up.

Isn't God amazing! I love how he operates—how he frees us from ourselves. Those first few years in Lebanon, God took me through what I describe as a death process. It felt like I was placed on an anvil and God was pounding and smashing out the selfishness, the pride, the fear, the stubbornness, and much more from me. It was a painful time with many tears shed, in large part because I felt so helpless.

And who ended up helping me? Most often it was the people I was sent to help. How humbling. I remember crying one evening and uttering the words to Carl, "When is life going to get easier?"

Carl simply responded, "Did Jesus have an easy life?"

It wasn't the sensitive answer I was looking for, but it was in alignment with what God was already doing in my life.

A Dutch friend of ours, who was working in Lebanon as an evangelist, was in our home one evening. Sensing my state, he asked me, "Do you remember Jesus' words about the kernel of wheat?" He knew I needed to hear them, so he proceeded to recite John 12:24: "Unless a kernel of wheat falls to the ground and dies, it remains only a single seed. But if it dies, it produces many seeds."

It took me a while to grasp the significance of the words Jesus spoke in this passage. The Lebanese were killing me with their kindness. And as a mom, I needed to deal with my selfishness. It was a struggle to give up my time for our three children, especially with Carl being so busy and not home much. I needed to trust God and lean heavily on him.

I eventually realized I was praying for the wrong things. Instead of praying for an easier life, I should have been praying for a life full of God. In my early days of following Jesus, I was kind of insular. I lived with a wall of protection around me just like a protective seed coat on an actual seed. I chose what I wanted to do rather than respond to what God was calling me to do. I gradually learned that sometimes I just had to dive in and not be afraid to get into things that appeared muddy to my own eyes. When you peer through God's lenses, you see that he makes all things beautiful. Serving beyond my comfort zone caused me to cry out to God for his help, and when I did, I experienced and saw incredible miracles. His love poured into me in unbelievable ways. Stepping out in baby steps or giant leaps when responding to God's call started to crack open that protective seed coat, and my death to self started to happen.

I had gone to Lebanon with my American identity, feeling pretty capable and sure of myself. I am so glad that God transformed my life and set me free from myself. I am thankful for my heritage, but it is just a sidenote compared to living as a daughter of the God of the universe. These days I feel less afraid, well loved, and freer, with more compassion for people who are hurting. Before, I was a happy, well-protected tiny seed just bouncing around doing my own thing. Now God's love and blessings are hard to contain, so I guess that's God at work, producing many seeds.

I drew a small picture of how God transformed me.

"Very truly I tell you, unless a kernel of wheat falls to the ground and dies, it remains only a single seed. But if it dies, it produces many seeds." (John 12:24)

Khalil Gibran, a famous Lebanese artist, poet, and writer, has something to say about this: "Of life's two chief prizes, beauty and truth, I found the first prize in a loving heart and the second in a laborer's hand."

As I allowed God to transform me and fill my heart with his love, my life began bearing fruit that lasted.

The W-Word
vs.
Helpful Information

Christ lives in me. And how great the difference! Instead of bondage, liberty; instead of failure, quiet victories within; instead of fear and weakness, a restful sufficiency in Another.

Hudson Taylor

Worry often feels legitimate. It many times comes packaged as "information": "We don't want to worry you, but seriously, have you seen how Muslims are expanding in the West? And did you see that YouTube video about shariah law and how they all want to control Europe and America? And they are growing like crazy, so I can see it happening! Really. We're just saying—you need to be informed."

Worry (fear's half brother) brilliantly masquerades as helpful information.

It's also cleverly disguised as "wisdom." I can't count how many times I have heard, "Yeah, but . . . Carl, are you sure that's wise?" I call *worry* the "W-word."

I remember when a well-meaning, godly leader in our church came to us a few months before Chris and I were about to move overseas. It was the end of 1991. The sixteen years of horrific civil war in Lebanon had ended just ten months earlier, and we were selling everything and taking our one-year-old and soon-to-be-born second child to Beirut.

Beirut. Where Terry Anderson, Thomas Sutherland, Terry Waite, and dozens of other hostages had just been released after years in captivity. The place was in ruins. And we were moving there—without even visiting first.

"Not very wise," said this good friend.

I remember smiling at him, not sure what exactly to say. I finally responded, "You're probably right." I could see his confused look as I turned to walk away, as if he were thinking, *So . . . you're still going?*

We went.

So how do we know when something really is helpful information or godly wisdom as compared to irrational worry or even fearmongering? The question to ask yourself is this: Is this an unreasonable, unhealthy fear that leads to a wrong response, or is this a helpful bit of information and godly wisdom that I need to learn?

Helpful information and godly wisdom will lead to positive action, freedom, loving others, faith, and hope. Fear that breeds worry, on the other hand, will lead to paralysis, hatred, anger, irrational decisions, and avoidance of those you're called to love.

The "Worry vs. Helpful Information" Test

Helpful information and godly wisdom will lead to:

Positive action (something productive and positive will result)

Freedom

Loving those we are called to reach

Faith and hope

Fear that breeds worry will lead to:

Paralysis

Hatred or anger toward others

Irrational decisions based on unreasonable conclusions

An avoidance of the ones we are called to reach

So which is from God? Seems fairly clear. Reject one. Embrace the other. If you honestly run everything through the above filter, you will almost immediately recognize which is crazy, worry-based fear and which is normal, healthy, get-out-of-Dodge fear. Remember this little acronym:

F—False

E—Evidence

A—Appearing

R—Real

So what's the secret to overcoming fear, whether it's a fear of flying or public speaking or traveling to Timbuktu? It's simple. You say yes.

But know that it's the first yes, followed by a string of yeses, that actually leads somewhere. You can never go from here to there in a single Superman bound. Still, it's the first yes that changes everything.

There's a great example of false evidence and unhelpful reporting in the book of Numbers. Moses and the children of Israel had come from Egypt and were at the border of Canaan—the land that had been promised to them. Moses asked Joshua and one representative from each of the twelve tribes to go and spy out the land and bring back a report. His instructions were specific:

- See what the land is like—give a general report.
- Are the people few or many? Strong or weak?
- Is the land itself good or bad?
- What are the towns like? Unwalled, or fortified?
- Is the soil fertile with trees?

After exploring the land for forty days, the spies brought back some of its fruit and gave a thorough report. Listen to this:

They first acknowledged that the land was, in fact, full of good and plentiful fruit. But they immediately went into fear mode. Numbers 13, verses 28 to the end, is a litany of "facts" provided by these concerned reporters.

Here's the gist of the rest of the report: "The people are huge and powerful. They are the descendants of Anak (who was the descendant of the Nephilim—and we all know who *they* are). The cities are large and fortified." The spies continued: "We can't attack those people; they are stronger than us. The land devours those living in it. All the people are of great size and we seemed like grasshoppers in our own eyes—and we looked the same to them."

Notice the shift? The spies went from reporting what they saw to a personal commentary based on their fears. If the Canaanites were so scary and so certain to kill them, how did the spies know they looked like grasshoppers to the Canaanites? Why weren't the spies devoured?

I see this fear perception almost every day in news reports. Even from our pulpits sometimes. We take some set of facts, work them through our preconceived idea about the situation, and spit out a scary potential commentary. If it was a formula, it might go like this: Facts on the Ground plus my Prejudice and Fears equal Something Very Scary!

Joshua wasn't buying. Presumably he saw the same things as the other twelve. But as he reports in the book named after him: "I brought . . . back a report according to my own convictions, but my fellow Israelites . . . made the hearts of the people melt in fear. I, however, followed the LORD my God wholeheartedly" (Joshua 14:7–8).

Love, love, love that. The others spread "a bad report" among the people, as it says back in the Numbers passage (13:32). They wanted everyone to join in their fear. Fear always seeks company. And it worked—fear sells.

But Joshua knew better. This land of Canaan had been promised to them, so why be afraid? Fear exaggerates, but faith breeds wisdom. Notice that Joshua didn't oppose their report; he didn't say it was untrue. He simply ignored it and said, "Surely we can take this land." And what did he base his statement on? His conviction—his faith—that God would do what he said he would do.

So Joshua said yes. But the people said no. And because of that, they wandered in the desert until every one of them died except Joshua and Caleb. A harsh treatment indeed, but it seems that God doesn't want us to be afraid. He tells us this over and over in Scripture. He welcomes our yes.

Okay, so I still haven't said yes to diving. I'm not sure I ever will. Well, I might dive into a swimming pool or even get certified. But headfirst into the depths of a dark, spooky ocean? Not likely.

Here's another confession (besides my fear of deep, dark places with man-eating animals): I've lived much of my life wanting to be like so-and-so. To have what he has. To be what he is. To write or speak the way he or she writes or speaks. When I read a book by Anne Lamott, for instance, I'm left thinking that I don't know the English language. When I hear

Billy Graham or Tony Campolo preach, I feel like a mumbling fool. When I read the theology of N. T. Wright, I'm confused as to how he got to know so much, while I can barely tie my soteriological shoes. I want to be where these and other people are, and I want to be there now!

There are several problems with this, of course. The most obvious is that I'm not any of those people and never will be—and shouldn't be. The second issue is that I can't get there from here. Well, unless I commit to 10,000 hours of practice, says Malcolm Gladwell.

Have you read Gladwell's book *Outliers: The Story of Success*? Great read. After finishing it, I had two main takeaways as to why some people are major successes:

1. Luck (as many call it)—when you were born, your circumstances, your upbringing.
2. You practiced the thing you're now good at for at least 10,000 hours.

So if I'm going to learn to dive—and then actually go diving— I guess I need practice. If you are going to live life large and overcome your fears of "what if," then you'll also need practice. You won't overcome your fears overnight.

So am I saying that I *can* be Billy Graham, Anne Lamott, or N. T. Wright? Well, yes. I mean, no. I can't be any of them— literally (especially not Anne Lamott)—but I can do what they do in a "Carl" sort of way, with tons of practice. So what's keeping me from that? Maybe a perceived lack of time? Insecurity, which is pride upside down? Or just good old-fashioned raw fear?

Being thrown in jail really isn't that bad. At least not in Lebanon.

About a year after moving to Beirut, we were down on the corniche—the gorgeous palm-covered walkway on the Mediterranean shores that surrounds Beirut's peninsula—sharing the great news that Jesus came to love people exactly like these. I was leading about fifteen other Arabs in this simple endeavor. As foolish as it may have been, we were doing it with pure motives and good hearts. But the next thing I knew, the local police had rounded up all of us in a thirty-second span, as if we had flashing lights on our heads signaling who we were. They shoved us into the back of their paddy wagon and whisked us off to the downtown Beirut police station.

Fourteen of us sat in the main cell area while one was taken to a room and interrogated. Each person would return with the same story—they were told that the one before them had "confessed" and promised to never do this again. They kept me till last. When I went in, the man behind the desk said, "Sit down, Mr. Carl. We know all about you. You are the leader, and we must speak frankly and openly."

"Of course," I responded. "I'm happy to talk about anything you like." (I wasn't so sure of the "leader" title—I wanted to tell him that would be Jesus, but I wasn't sure he was up for the nuance.)

He went on to inform me that while Christians were welcome in Lebanon (nearly 30 percent of the country is Christian), evangelizing Muslims was not. He said such activity destabilized the country, and that when a foreigner like me engaged in evangelizing, it was particularly dangerous because "others" might take advantage of the situation and use it for their evil purposes. That was a theme we'd hear many more times throughout our years of traveling in the Middle East. It was never the person we were talking to who wished us ill, but those "others" who did, and thankfully the person in front of us was there to rescue us.

My interrogator continued: "Mr. Carl, we like you very much (also something I'd hear a hundred times from officials trying to make a certain point), but you must never do this again. Please just sign this paper saying you will never evangelize on the streets of Beirut again."

I had an inkling "never evangelize" meant I shouldn't change people's religion, turn them into "Americans," and instruct the new convert to be against his family and generations of tradition. But I wasn't sure what the alternative was, so I said, "I can't do that, sir. I have to keep evangelizing."

We were missing each other. I was saying I felt compelled to share this wonderful news that Jesus had come to set people free, and he was saying that I should stop trying to make his Lebanese compatriots into Americans. But I was new to such issues, and he wasn't a man of many words; he was just doing his job—getting crazies like me off the streets of Beirut.

Funniest thing, about halfway through our night in the Lebanese slammer, one of the guards walked in and asked if I'd like a beef or chicken shawarma. He was making a food run and just wanted to be a good host. Next thing you know, we were all munching on delicious sandwiches with enough garlic to make our next evangelistic efforts knock the person in front of us off their feet.

Soon after, they released us with a "Now, you know you shouldn't do this anymore," to which we all replied, "*Insha'allah*" (God willing).

Nothing like a night in an Arab jail.

The point is—even when some of the things we fear actually do happen, they're not always that bad.

Fertilizing the Middle East—Becoming a Fool for Christ

> In humility value others above yourselves.
>
> The apostle Paul to the Philippians

My biggest fear in life is looking stupid. I really don't enjoy looking like I don't know what I'm doing. I need to be (or at least appear to be) cool, confident, and collected at all times. I'm sure there's some childhood thing connected to this—I just haven't figured out what. Actually, now that I think about it—it must have been my parents' fault!

Recently, one of our kids told me that if I ever wrote an autobiography, I should call it *Fertilizing the Middle East: Weapons of Mass Destruction (WMDs) and International Incidents of Diarrhea*, or something like that. I must have more stories of loose bowels in inappropriate places and with the greatest possible amount of embarrassment than anyone else in the world.

But here's one thing I've learned: It's good to feel foolish at times. Each embarrassing situation I survive makes me less scared about what I'll face in the future.

Here's my all-time most embarrassing story:

I traveled from our home in Lebanon to Iraq in May 2001, three months before 9/11. Saddam Hussein was hosting a Muslim-Christian dialogue conference in Baghdad, and I was invited to attend. There were about fifty Westerners in total (mostly Christians), and the other 4,950 were Iraqis and other Arabs (mostly Muslim, but some from Christian backgrounds).

It was amazing. There were Chaldeans, Assyrians, Melchites, Greek and Roman Catholics, Maronites, Arminians, Orthodox, Sabians (followers of John the Baptist), Shi'ite, Sunni, and Druze. A few mainline Protestants and an evangelical or two rounded out the gathering.

The second day there was set aside to travel south and visit the ancient ruins of Babylon (about an hour south of Baghdad), and from there we were set to see the childhood home of the biblical patriarch Abram (later Abraham)—a day no one would want to miss. But I woke up that morning with the worst diarrhea humanly possible. I won't go into great detail; let's just say that I couldn't walk from point A to point B without an explosion. So I did what any clearheaded person would do in that situation—I ate some bread and cheese and got on the bus headed to the south of Iraq.

There were actually three large buses full of folks. The patriarch of the Assyrian church was in the bus behind mine. Also in the group were the archbishop of the Chaldean church, a few Catholic and Orthodox bishops from the region, several prominent Muslim clerics, and a handful of key leaders from Lebanon. It was sort of a "Who's Who in the Middle Eastern Religious World." (And me.)

Our bus was in the front.

The landscape south of Baghdad is sort of like the top of your dining room table. A desert without dunes. A pancake of sand. Flat. Bare. Empty.

And then it hit. Not slowly or gently. Not like "Uh-oh, I think I might need to pull over at the rest area and use the facilities," but like NOW! I ran to the front of the bus and told the driver I needed "to go." He wisely and slowly replied that there were no facilities on the bus or anywhere nearby. I managed to convince him in my Lebanese Arabic that these were details that didn't matter. Actually, I think he took one look at my face and yanked the bus to the shoulder, almost skidding to a stop.

Remember that there were two other buses? Well, they pulled over right behind us, surely wondering what bad thing had happened to our bus.

I shot out of the bus door like a rocket with extra fuel and ran west. But there was no place to run to. No trees. No bushes. Nothing. But as I ran, I spotted a small plant about fifty yards out, and I headed for that. I just made it. Dropped my drawers, mooned the buses, and let it rip. WMD.

Red-faced, I slowly walked back to my bus. My friends were howling with laughter. One had recorded the whole thing on video. Others took pictures. The Catholic archbishop of Iraq came up to me and offered Imodium. Others just looked down with a sympathetic "You poor lad" sort of face. I wanted to crawl into a hole and die.

And—that's it. Nothing redeeming here (as far as I can tell). No one met Jesus that day. No great breakthroughs. No deeper meaning. I was just sick the rest of the day. While they were walking around Babylon and visiting our great patriarch's house in Ur, I sat curled up in a ball, holding my stomach, trying my hardest not to explode. That's what I was doing in Iraq three months before 9/11.

So it's true—there are some WMDs in Iraq, and I know where they are!

But seriously, when I asked my Facebook friends what they were most afraid of, one of the top answers was what I just wrote about—feeling or looking stupid, appearing to be a fool.

So let's just take the "what if" off the table, because we *are* fools. If you've given your life to following Jesus, you're a fool. You'll say and do things that won't make sense to most people. You'll live your life, in many ways, totally counter to the culture.

We're all fools. The only question is, Whose fool are you?

And speaking of foolishness, wait till you read the next chapter about trying to take cookies to Syrian soldiers!

Cookies for Syrian
Soldiers and the
Reality of Fear

What is to give light must endure burning.

Viktor Frankl

Perfect love casts out fear.

The apostle John to
early followers of Christ

Like I've said, some fear is real. The emotion is connected to reality. You're at knife point, or your house is on fire, or your kid has gone missing. That sort of fear is real. God made our emotions—and fear is one of them. I've had several such incidents; some I share in this book.

- Taken in Saudi Arabia by the airport police on my way to Yemen because I didn't have a transit visa. Spent two days in a Saudi jail with a hundred Bangladeshi refugees. They took my passport. I missed my flight. I was all alone and scared.

- Kidnapped in Iraq at gunpoint and robbed. Scary!

- Had our van rushed by two young men with gasoline and matches; my family was with me—frightening.

- Thrown in jail twice in Lebanon for gathering large crowds and speaking about Jesus. As I mentioned earlier, this was actually less scary than it might sound, but it was scary for Chris because both times she didn't know where I was.

- Lost in the mountains of Colorado twice—with no food and no shelter. Once with my son, who was fourteen at the time, I wasn't sure we were going to make it.

- Had the windows knocked out of my van—while I was in it—with Chris and the kids watching. They thought I'd be shot, since the man had a gun. Terrifying for all of us.

And then there's the scariness of uncertainty. My first-ever airplane flight was when I was twenty. I flew alone to Amsterdam, Holland, then took two trains, a bus, and a taxi to the YWAM base where I was going to live for six months. I spoke no Dutch and was all alone—and afraid.

The births of our children were slightly scary for different reasons each time. The first, well, was scary because it was the first. The second was because we had no money, so Marie was born in a public hospital with less than the best care. And the third—Jonathan—well, that was because he was born in Damascus on an August day when the temperature hit 105, and there was no air conditioning, and both Chris and Jon almost didn't make it—pretty good reasons to be scared.

Many of these times in my life have been when I was alone. Or have felt alone. Or when there was no way to know the outcome of a potentially dangerous situation. I doubt anyone reading the above examples would say, "Oh, come on, Carl. Get over it!" These are normal times to be afraid. And I agree.

But (and you had to know this was coming), it's what you do with your fear that matters. Being alone might make you feel lonely. It's what you do with that loneliness that matters. Feeling angry can be healthy. It's what you do with that anger that matters. Feeling frustrated, dissatisfied, confused, or disoriented are all normal emotions given to us by God. But it's what we do with them that matters. Where do they lead us? Do they control us? Do we obsess over them? That's when an otherwise normal negative emotion can become damaging—when we can't get it out of our head, when it keeps us awake at night.

When worry consumes us, it's an emotion out of control.

Chris and I had been in Beirut with our two baby girls exactly two days when we realized we could look out the bedroom window where we were staying and see a Syrian army camp. *Hmmm.*

"What are Syrians doing in Lebanon?" we asked our hosts.

A long monologue followed from our Christian-background Lebanese hosts about how the Syrians had taken over their country and were killing, raping, and pillaging without constraint. Basically, they tolerated them, because what else could they do? But not so secretly, the Lebanese despised the Syrian presence in their country. The Christian-background Lebanese were especially angry.

Chris and I didn't understand all the various nuances of hatred and rivalries that we'd stepped into. We just saw a bunch of tents with some lonely eighteen-year-old boys with guns. So we told our host family that we'd like to bake the soldiers some chocolate chip cookies.

Oh my. Did we ever get an earful. We didn't understand what these men had done, they told us. These may have been the very soldiers who had recently lined up thirty men in a nearby village and killed them, execution style, for no apparent reason. They wouldn't appreciate or understand our offer of kindness, our hosts went on to explain. The soldiers would think we were silly. Foolish. And who knows—maybe they'd kidnap us or worse. No, we should not do this.

We did it anyway.

Was it smart? Effective? Did it change the course of history? Nope—none of that. It did make our hosts mad. The Syrian soldiers did not laugh at us. They did like the cookies, however. They were appreciative. We learned some Arabic as we sat and ate with them. And—it helped us.

Frankly, after Chris and I had heard the horrible things about the soldiers, we were afraid. We didn't want to die two days after getting to Beirut. Actually, we weren't planning on dying at all, now that I think about it. We didn't want to offend our hosts, which we obviously would have (and did) by giving cookies to *their* enemies. We didn't want to be ignorant of the culture or do anything to embarrass ourselves or anyone else. There were lots of reasons not to do it. Besides, Syrians probably didn't eat chocolate chips in their cookies. (We've since noticed that *everyone* likes chocolate in their cookies. It could be the answer to world peace.)

But we realized that all these were simply excuses not to do something. It was just something simple. Not life-changing. Not earth-shattering. Not all that spiritual. We didn't share the Four Spiritual Laws with the soldiers or give them a *Jesus* film in Arabic or hand them a Bible. We just took them cookies on a plate with tinfoil over it.

It was a little awkward. We spoke no Arabic and they spoke no English. They had to be convinced it wasn't a trick, so I think I took one for the team and ate the first cookie.

But you know what it did do? It broke some of the fear gripping our hearts. This has become an ongoing lesson for us. When fear rears its ugly head, as it inevitably does, we don't succumb. When people tell us not to do this or that, we weigh their advice and sometimes go against it, since their advice is often based on their own fears projected onto us.

Chris

For our first five years in Lebanon, we lived in an apartment in the foothills of Beirut. The view from our balcony was beautiful. Each night we would watch the sun disappear into the Mediterranean Sea. Our apartment was surrounded by olive trees, as well as a few apricot, guava, almond, and fig trees. The kids have great memories of cracking almonds with rocks and munching on them, and eating fresh figs from the trees and sometimes even off the ground. They also had fun watching the olive harvesters come each year with their sticks that they used to bat down the olives onto a tarp that would be gathered up, taken away, and later turned into liquid gold. Sometimes we had the pleasure of watching a shepherd pass by with his sheep and goats. That particular memory is beautifully imprinted in my mind and gives greater meaning to the words "The Lord is my shepherd."

Not all days were serene and peaceful. I wrote the following during a time of unrest:

As the morning sun dawned over our home in the foothills of Beirut, I thought the day would be much like the weather appeared—clear, blue, and calm. Yet on this particular spring day in April, the serenity scattered from the sky above as the sun climbed higher and higher.

Suddenly, above the songs of the sparrows in the olive groves around our home and above the carefree giggles of the children playing in the garden, a new sound erupted—a thunderous boom. How could that be? The sky was a sea of brilliant blue.

As I ran out and surveyed the city of Beirut, which lay below us, I saw dark-gray billows of smoke rising above the concrete apartment buildings. Suddenly, I spotted Israeli helicopters coming in from the Mediterranean Sea. Another bomb was dropped, another deafening explosion.

Tears flowed down my cheeks as I thought of the cruelty of this attack. Terror seemed to choke out my breath as I raced outside to where the kids were playing and ordered them inside. They scurried into the house, surprised and confused by my reaction.

The earlier serenity of the blue sky was gone. The air raids intensified as the sounds of the incoming missiles were set to the backdrop of the helicopter's drone. I felt as if I could smell death and feel the horror of those being bombed just a few miles away.

Carl was in the city, seemingly in the very place where the Israelis were bombing. All I could do was pray for mercy and that he would return home!

The children carried on playing inside the house, oblivious to what was happening around them. However, I was nearly paralyzed with fear. As my tears flowed freely, I kept thinking, *Why do the Lebanese suffer continually? They have suffered through sixteen years of civil war—now this. Is it all beginning again? What is the purpose?*

As I realized the intensity of the moment, I was overcome with emotion: anger, frustration, a feeling of helplessness, and even guilt for being so disturbed by a few bombs when I knew our Lebanese friends had lived through this much of their lives. My heart was broken for this country, which was fast becoming ours, but I also was afraid for my own life and the life of my husband and children. Was that selfish, or normal?

The Israeli air strikes continued for sixteen long days. Day and night we could hear, see, and feel the explosions rocking the city of Beirut. Sadly, many people were killed and many more injured. We stayed and tried our best to comfort the many refugees who fled from the south, but we were overwhelmed by a sense of despair in the midst of tragedy. Our friends admired us for staying, I suppose. But it was no great act of courage—what else could we do? It was simply another day in the life of our Lebanese neighbors; for us, it was an event that changed the rest of our lives.

It's not possible to always be a Rambo or a Rocky. Lemons don't always make lemonade. Sometimes life is hard and scary things happen—then it gets worse. It might get worse, then better. Or it might just get worse and worse.

God our Father has our best in mind. He loves us and wants good things for us. At the same time, suffering, trials, and even persecution are promised. We don't look for them, we don't want or pray for them, but sometimes they happen. I have friends who spend a lot of time trying to figure out if these things are God's will, or allowed by God, or because of an evil, fallen world, or . . .

Me? Well, I'm a fairly simple guy. I just think bad things happen. And we respond one way or another.

It would be a malevolent God who would test and try us simply to see our response—or to have us "grow," as I often hear it described. So I don't think that's it either. Can we grow from hard times? Of course. Can God use tragedy and death and the worst things ever? Of course. He certainly did in this next story.

My friends Bonnie and Gary were missionaries in Sidon, Lebanon—the southern part of the country filled with Sunni Muslims. Sunnis are wonderful, loving families who work in orange groves during the day and fish for a living at night. Nearby are some of the most horrific camps of Palestinian refugees—people who used to live in what is now Israel. They live in total misery.

Bonnie was a prenatal nurse who served the poorest of the poor from both of these communities—Palestinians and Lebanese. Gary was the friendliest, most gregarious human on the planet. Everyone was his best friend. They had given their all for the sake of the good news. Or so they thought . . .

It was 7:30 on a Tuesday morning. My phone rang. It was my best friend, Dave. He was sobbing uncontrollably. I couldn't understand what he was saying. Or maybe it was that I didn't want to understand. Bonnie had been shot—in the head. In her clinic. She was dead.

Gary sprinted to the clinic that morning when he heard that something was wrong. *What can it possibly be? Is Bonnie okay?*

The police were already there, swarming the premises like ants. Gary burst through the door and saw the legs of his wife sticking out from the room off the entrance. With a gut-wrenching scream, he lunged toward her. Two cops tackled Gary and wrestled him to the floor, kicking and howling, "I want to see my wife! I want to see my wife!"

The police knew better. She had been shot point-blank in the face. They held Gary firmly to the ground. His head was a yard from her feet. He could see her blood.

The next day, I drove with Gary to the morgue to identify her body. He told me one thing was running through his mind. A song. A worship song simply titled "Surrender." In the awful aftermath of his wife's murder, my friend was silently singing to Jesus about surrendering everything to "know the lasting joy, even sharing in your pain."

Saying yes to Jesus always leads us on an adventure, but just in case you think I see the world through rose-colored glasses, well, you're wrong. I've been thrown in jail four times. We've had rocks thrown at us. There have been multiple death threats. My wife has been cursed at and my child spit upon. We've been kicked out of Lebanon not once, but twice. We have been held at gunpoint in Iraq and threatened by angry men with assault rifles who promised to kill us all if we didn't leave. Evil is real. Evil men exist. I've met some of them. I am not naïve.

But Gary paid the ultimate price. His wife was dead. They never found her killer, never knew the motive. When Gary stood three nights later in front of the world's TV cameras and forgave the man who killed his wife, that's when I knew that forgiveness is real. I always thought it was true, but that's when I knew it was. Forgiveness is possible. It's not some wimpy acceptance of someone's "I feel sorry for what I did; I'm sorry I hurt your feelings," but the real, intense forgiveness in the face of I-want-to-kill-you kind of evil. God really does have the power to change hearts. How else do you explain a devastated husband looking into the cameras next door to where his wife had just been murdered and saying the words "I love you. Whoever did this, I forgive you. Jesus died on the cross for you. And you can have new life in him." How else could a story like this happen? It is all true.

Was it persecution because Gary and Bonnie followed Jesus? Maybe. Trials and tribulations? Obviously. Suffering? Of the worst kind. But I'm not sure Gary was in the mood for a theological discourse on any of those issues. He still isn't. It happened—the most horrible thing imaginable. Did God work some good out of it? Well, yes. He always does. It's a promise. Was it his will or his allowed will for Bonnie to die like that? Wrong question. Bad questions like that lead to bad answers that cause us to make up an awkward theological response like "It wasn't God's perfect will, but he permitted it to show us his glory . . ." or something like that.

How about this, instead? For whatever reason—the world is fallen; there is sin, evil, our mistakes, the devil, whatever—bad stuff happens. Not sure it even matters why it happens. It just does. Life isn't always easy. Sometimes it's unbelievably hard, as it was for Gary. And then we're left with questions. And fear. Why? Why me? Was it my fault? Should we go home? Change course?

When I asked Gary a few months ago if I could share his story, here was his email reply: "Yes, Carl, if it will encourage people to work through fear. Fear is an interesting phenomenon, trying to understand what is real and what is just our perception. But it seems clear to me that we are mostly pacified by virtual or perceived fear. And as for death and the fear of death, my question is for those of us who want to live fully: 'Is what we're living for worth dying for?'"

And that's what we're left with—questions. It feels better to know the answers. But that's not real life. We don't always "know." We want to. We long to know, but it's more likely we're just left with questions. Good systematic theology tries its best to answer these mysteries, and we want so badly for them to be solved. It just feels better if we know why. But if we're honest, we often don't know why.

It's an adventure. We say yes. We sign up and we don't look back. Hands to the plow. Remember my definition of an adventure? A risky journey with an uncertain future. If we know all the answers, it's no longer a risk, and thus it's not really an adventure.

No adventure. No Jesus. They go together.

And things don't always turn out well. While we believe by faith that God is still good and that his desire for us is to bless us, there is no need for a simplistic platitude of the "God is good, all the time; all the time, God is good" variety. We do believe that is true, but we do not need to pretend we feel it or even understand it. Sometimes neither is possible. And that's okay. Actually, I'd say that's the boldest kind of faith. If we "know," then it isn't faith. Faith is assurance of what we don't know and what we can't see. Our faith is in God—not in our knowledge of God.

We refer to Hebrews 11 as "the faith chapter" in the Bible. It's full of amazing heroes of the faith: Abraham, Sarah,

Moses, Noah, David, Rahab, and Samuel, to name a few. The "Who's Who" of the Bible. Verse 1 through the first part of verse 35 includes some of the most awe-inspiring words of Scripture.

Then it takes an ugly turn. I don't hear many preach on the second part of verse 35 through verse 38:

> There were others who were tortured, refusing to be released so that they might gain an even better resurrection. Some faced jeers and flogging, and even chains and imprisonment. They were put to death by stoning; they were sawed in two; they were killed by the sword. They went about in sheepskins and goatskins, destitute, persecuted and mistreated—the world was not worthy of them. They wandered in deserts and mountains, living in caves and in holes in the ground.

I haven't heard a lot about the promise of getting sawed in half lately. No one is claiming that verse. We don't look for it. Don't expect it. Don't want it. But it might happen. It's part of the riskiness of the adventure.

In the weeks after Bonnie was killed, waves of fear swept over Chris and me. I know this is a book about working through fear but, well, this was different. Walking home at night, where we typically had felt safe, now seemed terrifying. Every sound I heard as I walked down our dark street was surely a gunman lurking in wait for me or Chris. A knock on the door was now from the butt of a pistol. Drivers too close to our car felt like men stalking us.

Raw fear. I could smell it. We added a lock to our door. Okay, to tell the whole truth, we added a door to our door. I brought in my old Palestinian friend who found a guy who knew a guy who had an uncle with a metal door company. Yep, we put a metal door on the outside of our door. With heavy hinges and a small peephole. We were scared.

How's that for honest? Some suggested we come back to the States. Take the kids out of school and just catch the next plane home, where we'd be safe from killers like Bonnie's.

But we didn't. We didn't go home. Lebanon *was* our home. Don't get me wrong—it wasn't easy to stay. We were afraid for a long time. And I can remember being afraid of feeling afraid. I was Carl of Beirut. Tough guy. Mr. No Fear himself. Not now, as I sit writing this book, but then. I was the guy who was never afraid. But then I was. And that made me feel awful. I hadn't lost my wife. Nothing had happened to me. But just the thought that something could happen almost paralyzed me.

But it didn't.

Storms

There are some things one can only achieve by a deliberate leap in the opposite direction.

Franz Kafka

For God has not given us a spirit of fear and timidity, but of power, love and self-discipline.

The apostle Paul to Timothy

They called it a hundred-year storm. It came at night with the fury of a hurricane, even though the Mediterranean isn't supposed to have hurricanes. The poor refugees—a mix of Syrian Bedouins, Arab Gypsies, and Palestinians—all living in shacks right on the beach, never knew what hit them. Many lost their lives, and several of their kids were washed out to sea never to be seen again.

I had never been there before. I didn't know these people, and had never even heard of them. They were truly some of the forgotten ones. But when you hear a story like this on the news, well, you have to act.

I went directly to one of the most powerful men in the country—a cabinet minister close to the president. I pleaded with him to allocate resources for these people, but all he said was, "God bless you, Carl. Do what you can, because the government does not acknowledge that they exist."

I went home, talked to Chris, called my buddy Dave and a couple of other friends, and took all our cash from my secret money drawer (which doubled as the place where I kept my underwear). Two thousand dollars. We filled our van and another one with blankets and food.

First thing the next morning, my family piled into the van, surrounded by boxes of food, and we drove to the beach. It was going to be a great day serving the poor. And doing it with my kids—man, was I ever a proud dad.

We drove down the hill to within a stone's throw of the water. The makeshift houses were gone, swept away. People were everywhere. Dazed, homeless, afraid, cold, and hungry. We were honored to be there helping them.

We jumped out of our van and let the folks know we had food for them. Boxes of it. And the van right behind us was full of blankets and some small cooking stoves. As you can imagine, the people were excited. Very excited.

Chris and the kids got out and walked back a ways with some friends to watch and help when needed. I stayed in the van for a minute to be sure it was in the best place to unload the boxes.

Suddenly there was a crowd. I don't know how it happened, but from nowhere, it seemed like a hundred people were packed around my van. And in the middle of it all was a man with a pistol. He waved it around wildly, and then he lunged at my window, breaking it with the butt of his pistol. It sounded like an explosion. Or like a shot.

My family had seen a man with a gun lunging at me, and they heard an explosion as well. They were sure I'd been shot. I thought I'd been shot. In fact, I sort of jerked forward against the steering wheel, feeling for my breath and wondering if I was dead. I realized I was not dead when I noticed all the same people around me, and I was sitting in the same spot in my van. But Chris and the kids didn't know that.

The man with the gun then broke out my side window and the rear window. Then people started grabbing boxes from inside the van. They were getting wilder and angrier by the minute. Suddenly my dear Palestinian friend, Jihad, threw open my door, grabbed me, and threw me to the other side. He jumped into the driver's seat and shouted, "Hold on—we're getting out of here."

He nearly ran over a dozen would-be box grabbers on his wild reversal out of that mob. We flew back up the road to the hilltop where my family was standing, crying. Did I mention it was raining?

Our friend Jihad screamed at my family to jump in the van, and we drove off—rain pouring in our broken windows with half-opened boxes leaking food while our hearts leaked pain. The Medearis Family Do-Good Trip had turned into a nightmare. Broken windows, broken hearts. People still wet and cold and hungry.

One of our daughters whispered faintly, "Daddy, do we have to go back there again?"

"No, honey. No, we don't."

No easy answers came that day. No religious assurances. No theological certainties. Just confusion and hurt and lots and lots of questions.

Bad things happen. And it doesn't always make sense. But Jesus still says, "Follow me." And we still say yes.

But why do we say yes to Jesus when life hurts? When it all goes bad and the storms pound us relentlessly? Is it because we're supposed to? Because it's God's will?

I remember growing up with the theology "If you don't obey God, then you're in sin—and we know where that leads—so you'd better obey!" Like all partial truths, this is partially true. It is good for us to obey (my term for "obey," if you haven't guessed, is to "say yes.") But obedience for the sake of obedience doesn't make that much sense and for sure doesn't resonate well with a younger generation that has been taught to question everything. They want to know, and they ought to know *why*.

Remember when Jesus gave his hard and slightly bizarre teaching in John chapter 6? Right in the middle of his otherwise very nice discussion about his being the bread of life, Jesus inserts this odd thing about eating his flesh and drinking his blood.

By the way, do you know that in the Arab world, one of the words in Arabic for *bread* is the same word for *life*? If you're at dinner and you ask your mom to pass the bread, you're also saying, "Pass the life." Cool, eh? So when Jesus is saying, "I am the bread of life" and he's speaking Aramaic, he's also being heard as saying, "I'm the life of life—I am life. If you have me, you have life."

But when Jesus makes it practical by saying they must eat and drink him, well, that freaks some of them out, and they leave. He then does this wild thing (which I never do, by the way, when someone leaves me): he turns to the others and asks if they want to leave, too. They probably do, but Peter jumps up and says, "Yeah, but to whom should we go? Only you have the words of life."

See, Peter got it (this time at least). Life can be tough. Jesus' teachings are not always easy to understand. Maybe we want to leave or quit or move on to something else—something that makes more sense, frankly. But we sort of know down inside that there's something special about Jesus. That he's the One and Only. He is full of both grace and truth. He holds the key to both life and death, to good and bad. And somehow, we know that he's trustworthy. So we follow. We say yes. Even when it doesn't make sense.

Chris

After our first two years in Lebanon, we were about to have our third child. Because the American embassy was still closed from the war, we had to decide where we were going to deliver our baby so that a passport would be issued to our new child. We had friends in Syria at the time, and a place was offered for us to stay if needed, so we said yes. After just a two-hour taxi drive, we were in Syria and we started the waiting.

The delivery was difficult—touch-and-go at times. A small hospital nearby was experiencing technical difficulties and had to shut down, creating an overflow of people in our hospital. Not only was the hospital overcrowded, but the air conditioning puffed its last breath of cool air and then ceased to work. It was the middle of August, and the outside air temperature was sweltering. During the delivery, I remember reciting Psalm 23 in my head as things became difficult. I felt like I was walking near the valley of the shadow of death. I felt afraid, yet Psalm 23 kept me hanging on. We also had a good friend who had come to the hospital and was praying right outside the doors. Eventually our little boy was born, but the room was silent. He wasn't breathing. They took him over to a little table and administered oxygen for what seemed like an eternity. Then the room resounded with a cry, and I immediately started to cry, as well. Carl and I were so excited to have a new baby, and it was a great surprise to have a precious little boy.

After leaving the hospital and returning to our friends' home, I began to be concerned about Jonathan's eyes. They looked strange to me. The whites of his eyes were completely wine-colored. The doctor gave me a small bottle of drops to put in his eyes. After taking a nap one afternoon, I picked up Jonathan from his crib, and when he cried, I noticed his tongue was brown. *Oh no! Now what is wrong?* Marie, our second child, must have sensed my concern, because she proudly told me, "Mommy, I gave Jonathan his whole bottle!" She then handed me the empty bottle of eye-drop solution. The poor little thing thought she was being helpful by dousing her new brother's eyes with the drops.

Carl had to travel to Europe just a few days after Jonathan was born, so I shuffled about and did the best I could with the kids. One day, when the girls were a little stir-crazy from being housebound, we ventured out and took a taxi to a park. There I was thrilled to find a bench near the jungle gym, where I could watch Anna and Marie work off some energy. Not long after, an Arab family walked by me and said hello. I learned they were visiting from Kuwait and that the gentleman was a pediatrician. Still desperate to know about the condition of Jonathan's eyes, I asked the doctor if he would mind sharing his opinion. He gently took Jonathan in his arms and looked into his eyes. He then asked about the birth, if it had been traumatic, and I replied with a definite yes. Hearing that, the doctor assured me that Jonathan's eyes would clear up in a few more days. It felt like a hundred pounds had been lifted from my shoulders, and I thanked the family profusely. Yet again God had sent someone to help me just when I needed it! Leaving the park that day, I had a spring in my step and restored hope in my heart.

God is amazing.

Fear Sells

Perfect love, we know, casts out fear. But so do several other things—ignorance, alcohol, passion, presumption, and stupidity. It is very desirable that we should all advance to that perfection of love in which we shall fear no longer; but it is very undesirable, before we have reached that stage, to allow any inferior agent to cast out fear.

C. S. Lewis

Confess your sins to one another . . . that you may be healed.

James in his letter to the twelve tribes

've already mentioned the thought that fearmongering often disguises itself as helpful information. Certain media outlets are worse at this than others, but they all thrive on this form of entertainment: "Be worried, be very worried, because _____."

Just think about how much time has been consumed with whether President Obama has a U.S. birth certificate or whether he is a Muslim. I'm not a fan of all of his policies, but imagine this: He keeps saying, "I'm a Christian," and gives a clear testimony of his faith (which I've personally heard several times), and yet certain Christians keep saying, "Nope, you're a Muslim." Imagine any other person saying, "I'm a Christian," and then all the Christians saying, "No, you're not—you're a Muslim." What a bizarre phenomenon, all stirred by certain media outlets that seem to take a specific interest in playing to the fears of its audience.

A month ago, I received an email that was being passed around saying that the "bad-guy" Muslim Brotherhood was now in fourteen top-level positions in our government (of course, appointed by President Obama). I looked at every supposed person listed. First of all, most were not Muslim Brotherhood at all (two were, and they were both still in Egypt). The others were random Muslims from India or other places—not even living in the U.S. I actually knew a couple of them, and they were the furthest thing imaginable from being a bad-guy Muslim Brotherhood person.

I've heard for years now that Obama is the first U.S. president since Dwight Eisenhower to not attend the National Prayer Breakfast that is held each February in Washington, D.C.—that he attends the annual Ramadan Iftar for Muslims, but not the National Prayer Breakfast. Strange, because I've personally seen him at the prayer breakfast each year of his presidency. But when someone wants to believe something, they don't need any actual evidence to support their view.

How about the emails and YouTube videos that have gone viral over the years about how Muslims are going to be the majority in Europe by the year 2025? Again, it's media playing on our fears. In this case, it's not even true. The United Kingdom is about 5 percent Muslim. France and Germany (the countries with the most Muslims in Europe) are about 15 percent. It is true that the Muslims in those countries are more likely to have a higher birthrate than the white Europeans, so maybe someday, in a couple of hundred years, there could be more Muslims in Europe—but who knows?

Here's an interesting irony. Follow closely:

- These emails and YouTube videos are often produced and propagated by concerned evangelical Christians in the West.
- At least theoretically, these very Christians would want to lead these Muslims to Jesus.
- France, Germany, and the U.K. are some of the least-Christian places on earth. Most of the white Europeans who live there are non-churchgoing agnostics.

It seems that we'd rather a country like France remain fully postmodern and non-Christian than become a bit more God-fearing as a result of an increase of Muslims. Since when did we become so interested in preserving pagan postmodern French culture? The answer seems to be—as soon as France started becoming more Muslim.

I think this exposes some kind of serious anti-Muslim issue we have here. It appears to be preying on something deep within us.

Bottom line is this: We're afraid of Muslims. And fear is a powerful motivator.

Or, switching gears a bit, do you remember the Malaysian jet that disappeared in 2014? It really wasn't a U.S. interest story from either a personal or political standpoint, yet our news covered it night and day for weeks. Why? Fear. It played on some latent fear we all have of flying or maybe of disappearing.

Fear sells. I have often joked that if my first book had been called *Muslims, Christians, and the Coming Jihad,* it would have sold even more copies (instead of "the Coming Jihad," it has "Jesus" in the title, in case you're wondering).

A certain U.S.-based twenty-four-hour news channel has run this banner at the bottom of its page for years: "The War on Terror." The message to viewers? We're at war. There are terrorists out there. Be careful. Be wise. Be vigilant. Be informed. Remain afraid.

One more example, and this is a tough one to even dare to bring up: children abducted in the United States. Even one is too many. Strangers abducting children, who are then lost (in one form or another), has averaged less than fifty a year. Out of 313 million people, that's an incredibly small percentage. About the same number that die each year from lightning strikes.

There's something scary about randomness. Fear of the unknown—of the what-ifs—is the worst kind of fear. What *might* happen can consume us. And, of course, those are the kinds of things that keep our twenty-four-hour news channels in business.

Obama's Muslim agenda. Terrorism. Muslims taking over the world. Missing airplanes. Missing children. All random. All scary.

If you want to be honestly scared of something, try these:

1. In the U.S., in 2012, 34,000 died from auto accidents.

2. About 600,000 die each year from heart disease.

3. About 130 are killed each year in the U.S. by hitting a deer on the road with their car. (An average of one U.S. citizen is killed every year by a shark.)

But which are you more afraid of—deer or sharks?

Fear of public speaking (really, what's the worst that can happen?); fear of flying; fear of spiders and snakes, of heights; fear of the dark—these are our biggest worries? *Really?*

I'm hoping to show you how silly most of our fears actually are. They're ridiculous. Recognize that. Admit it. Make fun of them! Tell the world that you used to be afraid of these things, even though you don't know anyone who ever died from any of them. (Saying this, I'm sure that someone will, in fact, know someone who has died of a spider bite or snakebite, or fell off a cliff or something—to you, I am very sorry.)

So what do we do with these "silly fears"? Well, it's simple, really . . .

Surely you're one of the millions who have watched Bob Newhart play a no-nonsense therapist in his famous "Stop It" video.* Newhart's only response to every problem the woman mentions is to "stop it."

So that's my advice for being afraid of the dark, of spiders, snakes, planes, failure, heights, etc. *Stop it.*

See how easy that was? You're healed.

Okay, so maybe that doesn't always work. But actually, sometimes it does. I'd start there. Try this simple exercise.

First, you must identify *what* you're afraid of. Seriously, take five to ten minutes right now and do a "fear inventory." I've listed several common ones already, but let me make a fuller list right now, just to help you get going. You have to be honest for this to work.

Fears!

Flying. Public speaking. Heights. The dark. Intimacy. Water. Closed spaces. Death. Failure. Rejection. Spiders. Snakes. The unknown. Being lost. Commitment. Terrorism. Fire. Lack of

*If you haven't seen the Newhart video, take five minutes and watch it now at https://www.youtube.com/watch?v=Ow0lr63y4Mw&feature=kp.

security. Lack of finances. Marriage. Children. Kidnapping. Losing your freedom. Severe pain. Disappointment. Loneliness. Needles. Being seriously sick.

You can fill in the others. Write them out on a piece of paper. Every one. Maybe even try listing them from most serious to least worrisome.

(Elevator music playing)

Did you do it? If not, stop—please do it.

Done? Okay, now here's what we're going to do next. This is getting scary, I know—maybe you need to add "reading this stupid book" to your list of things you're afraid of.

Get a friend, your spouse, or just someone who knows you well and whom you can trust. Tell them what you're doing, and read your list of fears out loud to them. Ask them not to counsel you, just to listen. And you don't need to explain your fears—just read them.

Mine would be deep water, rejection, lack of significance, and snakes. Man, do I hate snakes. Of course, I'm justified in that one since Satan appeared as a snake. Oh wait, sorry. We're not explaining or justifying. Forgot my own advice.

So, you've written them down and shared them with a friend. Promise me you've done that before you keep reading. Put the book down and do that now.

I'm assuming an hour, a day, or a week has gone by since you read that last line. Correct? You've now read your fears out loud to someone you know and trust. How did that feel? What was their reaction? Anything interesting or surprising?

Okay, that was all Step #1: You've identified and confessed your fears—a huge step toward being free.

Step #2: Try to identify where these fears came from. I'm not a psychologist or even a basic counselor, so nothing out of the ordinary here. Just spend time thinking about why you might be afraid of those things. There might be some actual reasons, and it'd be helpful for you to know them. Like, you're afraid of spiders because one bit you when you were a kid and you had a reaction to it. Or of heights because you fell from the second story of your house while sneaking out of a window late one night as a teenager. You get the picture.

By the way, a very important interlude here: If while doing these exercises you realize you have some deep issues you need help with, well, get help—actual help from a trained professional. A pastor or counselor should at least be able to point you in the right direction.

Okay, you've identified your fears and where they came from, and you've shared them with someone; now here's what I recommend for Step #3: If you think about it for a minute, you'll know what I'm going to say: Jesus. Jesus works.

So here's what you do (but only do this if you're serious about actually getting rid of your fears and phobias): Grab that trusted friend—or someone else you respect and trust—and ask them if they'd be willing to help set you free from your fears. If you're afraid to ask someone to help with this—well, then I don't know what to say. Just stop it—ask someone! If they know you and know Jesus, they're good enough. They do not need to be a trained professional to do this; they need to know and love you, and know and love Jesus. That's it. For real.

Share with your friend your fears (even if you have already done so with the same person, do it again) and why you think you might be afraid of these things. Obviously, honesty is what will make this work. Be brutally honest. Share as much as you can think of. This could take five minutes or five hours. Take as much time as you need. Do it in two evenings or a weekend, whatever you need. Jesus isn't going to get busy and leave you. Take your time.

Have your friend go through the list with you and pray for you about each fear. There's no need for long, fancy prayers. Regular, normal prayers will do just fine (maybe better).

Acknowledging a fear could go something like this: I have a fear of dying because my grandma died when I was very young and I was there. So I've always been afraid to die.

You've now recognized the fear, identified where it came from, and confessed it to a friend. That's going a long way toward healing already. Now your friend will pray for you.

They might ask Jesus to show you that he was there with you in that painful moment. They might invite the Holy Spirit to be present as they pray. They might ask God the Father to show you how much he loves you and cares for you in your pain.

In case you're wondering, I'm not writing this haphazardly or in a frivolous manner. I have personally experienced this kind of healing. Chris and I learned about this kind of help during a five-day intense, personal retreat called "Healing for the Nations," based in Kansas City. The foundation for much of what they do is based on 2 Corinthians 10:5: "We demolish arguments and every pretension that sets itself up against the knowledge of God, and we take captive every thought to make it obedient to Christ."

You and I can't demolish the arguments against us from our enemy or take thoughts captive if we don't know what those arguments and thoughts are. People often go through life not taking the time to identify them. It seems silly to me now, except I must admit that I didn't identify my own fears for many years. Not until one good friend—Floyd McClung of YWAM, now of All Nations—told me I had to go to this retreat (in no uncertain terms and with no out-clause). I went. Chris followed. And it changed our lives.

Identifying our fears, naming them, and then confessing them has enormous power. And when we pray for healing, we are delivered. I fully expect, if you have listed your fears, confessed them, and had someone pray with you about them, that you too are now free from the fears that plagued you.

You might think this chapter should have been placed at the end of the book, or as an addendum. I could have called it "Where Do We Go From Here?" or "Three Easy Steps to Freedom." But here's why I put it in the middle of the book: We have to get used to living as free people. Being spiritually set free and walking out that freedom on a daily basis are two different things.

Imagine what a fear-free life now looks like. "No Fear" is not a logo but a banner over your life. We are free to be free. Galatians 5:1 says: "It is for freedom that Christ has set us free. Stand firm, then, and do not let yourselves be burdened again by a yoke of slavery." Paul seems to know that even though we've been set free, we can still choose to walk again in bondage.

Why would we do that? Why would you, when you know you've experienced real freedom, choose to walk again in slavery? Well, I think there are a couple of reasons:

1. The old ways are familiar. We feel comfortable there; it's what we know. It's how we think.

2. With new freedom comes new responsibility. It's easy being a slave. You have very few choices when you're in captivity. Freedom is open and confusing, and you've never been there before. You may experience new fears now that you're free.

3. Most people around you are not free, so you may feel odd. It's actually not all that "normal" to be free. Without being judgmental, most of our friends and family are in bondage to their own sets of fears, and you've become used to relating to them in that way.

So some of us choose to go back to bondage, even when we've been set free. And you know what? It's okay. Don't beat yourself up over it. You can be free again. And again. And then again. There's no end to the grace of freedom.

Just remember, it's for freedom you have been set free. In other words, you are free to be free (rather than live in bondage). You might as well choose the way of freedom. It is the way of Jesus.

The Kids Didn't
Choose This

He is no fool who gives what he cannot keep to gain what he cannot lose.

Jim Elliot

Let the children come to me.

Jesus

Okay, here's a gut check for all adults who choose to follow this adventurous way of Jesus: Your kids might pay a price they didn't sign up for. And it's not really fair.

As you know, our girls were very young when we moved to Lebanon in July 1992. They were just seventeen months and four months old. They didn't agree to leave Colorado Springs and move to Beirut. Actually, now that I think of it, Chris and I did ask them—they just didn't have much to say!

All of our kids' first memories were of Lebanon. Most of their friends were Lebanese. They thought tabouli was the salad everyone ate and that hummus should be at every meal. They only knew bread that looked like a smooshed American pancake—flat and round. It's funny, but we asked our kids a few years ago, after we'd been back in the States awhile, if they remembered the large Lebanese army tank that sat in front of their school's entrance. None of them did. They thought we were joking.

Can you imagine not remembering a tank with a guy on top manning the turret machine gun—right in front of your school, every single day? What they did remember was the man selling round pocket bread called *kaikh* and another who sold seasoned fava beans. Those two stands were five feet from the army tank. Funny what we remember and don't remember.

Our son, Jonathan, spoke Arabic so naturally that when one of our American friends asked him if he spoke Arabic, he said, *"La"* (which is "no" in Arabic). He didn't even know he spoke Arabic. Our kids' schools were taught in English, French, and Arabic, all mixed together. The teachers would go in and out of all three languages. Our kids thought it was normal.

I remember one time Chris and I decided to visit some Bedouins (semi-nomadic Arabs) who lived over the mountains toward Syria in the Beka'a Valley. We decided our kids should come along and bring a few of their toys to give to these poor children. It was a hilarious moment when they chose to part with almost all of their most expensive toys. It was no big deal for them, but it did challenge Mom and Dad's faith.

We piled into our car with a couple of friends from the States and drove the hour and a half over the gorgeous Lebanese mountains into the Beka'a Valley. We had no great plan. In fact, I remember driving around until we saw a group of tents, where we pulled up and got out of the car to an almost immediate mob of curious kids. The adults weren't far behind, but the kids came first.

We'd been in Lebanon only about a year, so our Arabic was pretty bad. We tried to explain that we had come in the name of Jesus and wanted to help in any manner possible. We opened our car trunk and starting passing out the toys—which quickly became a chaotic disaster when the older kids started beating up the younger ones and taking the toys. Our kids got scared and wanted to get back in the car. Instead, we had a brilliant idea: Let's sing them a song in Arabic. Can't remember why, but we chose one that you might remember from Sunday school. It goes like this: "I have the joy, joy, joy, joy, down in my heart. Where? Down in my heart."*

There was one problem—in Arabic, the words *joy* and *mouse* sound a lot alike. We didn't know the difference and couldn't really properly pronounce the word *joy*, which has a unique vowel in it, so we sang *"mouse"* (not knowing, of course). You can imagine the kids' puzzled look as we sang about the mouse in our heart. *Where's the mouse? It's in our hearts.* Wow!

Other than the fact that the kids didn't fully appreciate our kids' most expensive toys, and that the adults were suspicious of us, and that we sang about a mouse in our hearts, the time went fairly well. And because it did, we took similar trips several other times with our kids. We got a little better at Arabic and learned what was helpful and what wasn't. But at no point did an all-out Jesus movement start because of our feeble efforts. Mom and Dad were just saying yes to what we thought God was asking of us, and our kids followed.

In 1993, about a year after we settled in to our new home in Beirut, we did something called a "March for Jesus." A British fellow named Graham Kendrick was doing these around the world, and we volunteered to lead the one in Beirut with a Lebanese worship band. We tried to get permission from the city but couldn't, so we did what any responsible citizen would—we did it anyway. About a hundred of us—maybe seventy Lebanese and thirty foreigners—walked and sang and

*Watch and hear the song "Down in My Heart" at https://www.youtube.com/watch?v=69-d5N01Wrg.

prayed right through the old green zone (the line between east and west Beirut during the civil war years). We gathered at the end of the street and held a worship concert right there. Several hundred gathered to watch, all a bit confused as to what was happening. Then the police came. I remember a grim-looking captain asking me what we thought we were doing and if we had a permit. I told him we were asking God to bless Beirut and Lebanon and singing praise and worship songs to God and thanking Jesus for how awesome he is.

I'll never forget his response: "Oh, well, okay then."

That was it. And our kids were with us.

One thing Chris and I learned fairly early on was that if we treated things as normal, then others would also see them as normal. Don't get me wrong—we had plenty of Saturdays where we just went to the beach. Other days, the kids would wake up and watch cartoons and then figure out if they were going to their friends' houses or if their friends were coming to ours, or if we were all going camping in the mountains or swimming at the pool, or . . . just like your family. But as often as possible, we'd involve our children in what we were doing.

On Tuesday nights, we'd have a bunch of students over, mostly from the American University of Beirut. They were all Lebanese, but they spoke English fluently—some as their first language. We'd worship together and study the Scriptures. We always invited our kids to join us, and they usually did.

On Friday nights, we'd all go to our community center, called the "Olive Grove," to play Ping-Pong, pool, and foosball, and then sing and study the Scriptures. There would be anywhere from twenty to a hundred of us. Our kids were invited, and they always went. They'd stay with us sometimes and other times go in the back with their friends and do a mini version of what we were doing. But it was all one big family. Our kids loved going to the Olive Grove—a five-block walk from our downtown Beirut flat.

As they got a little older, Chris started something called the "Kids' Club." I'll let her tell you about that.

Chris

After five and a half years of living in the foothills of Lebanon, we decided to move down to the center of Beirut. I was a little apprehensive but felt like God was again stirring our hearts to respond to another adventure. We found an apartment that had a pretty good-sized balcony that we thought could be transformed into a little garden for our children. We put down a piece of green artificial turf, built a little jungle gym on top, and, presto, the balcony became a fun play place. Their friends loved to visit our fourth-floor playground.

When Anna, Marie, and Jonathan got older, I knew I wanted to do more with the community. I became friends with many Muslim women, and as our friendships deepened, I asked if they would like to study the Bible and pray, and they agreed. We usually met and chatted over a cup of coffee and pastries, studied passages from the Bible, and then prayed. We usually prayed for our families, especially the children.

I also started the Kids' Club, which met every Friday night. We were given a nice facility that was big enough for kids to run around in and have fun, while also hearing stories about Jesus. Most of the children who came were Muslim, so we asked for permission from the families, and they agreed to send their children. All of these families are still, to this day, close friends of ours.

One Friday night in late March, during Kids' Club, we were having fun playing floor hockey, when our time was interrupted by one of the parents who was a good friend of mine. She came in and hugged her daughter. I noticed her eyes starting to tear up. She told us she had just been at the hospital, and that a boy from their school had been run over by a taxi. The doctors didn't think he was going to make it. My whole body was stricken with grief. Then in the next desperate moment, I had an overwhelming surge of faith. "We should pray right now for this young boy to be healed," I said.

My friend was herself a doctor, and her response signaled her apparent resignation about the boy's condition. "Pray if you like," she said, "but I need to be going."

I got into a little circle with some of the children and said, "Let's just talk to God and ask him to heal this little boy."

Each child watched me cry and ask for God's mercy to heal the boy. Then one by one, the children proceeded to ask God in their own tender little voices to intervene and heal this boy. This was a time when I felt like God heard our cries and came and touched the very place where we were.

The young boy did not die that evening. He did, however, go into a coma. We soon found out that this little boy was in our middle daughter's class. We continued to pray. Their Lebanese teacher, who had such a sweet disposition, would visit him every day and sit by his bedside and read to him. Time passed. Prayers continued. Then on the last day of school, our daughter Marie and her classmates had a surprise visitor. You can only guess who it was.

Our kids love Lebanon. They love God. They even love us! We aren't perfect parents, and they haven't always been perfect kids, but they think sharing their faith is normal and that living the adventure of following Jesus is normal, as well. They didn't originally choose this path, but now they have.

I'm not sure I can back this up with any verifiable data, but I often wonder if the crazy rapid growth of extreme sports and of wild reality TV shows has something to do with our raising a generation that is often bored. Their real lives aren't very interesting, and parents are overly busy, so they need to find entertainment via the Internet, TV, or Xbox, or by taking on physical challenges through extreme sports.

What if we parents were better at creating an atmosphere of adventure for them as we follow Jesus together as families? Not in a weird hyper-religious manner, but in a real, earthy, everyday sort of way that makes doing cool Jesus things exciting. That's been our family's goal. And you can ask our three now-adult children if it worked. I'll let them answer for themselves (and share the good and the bad).

Anna

It was May 2003, just two months after the U.S. had gone into Iraq. We were living in Lebanon at the time, and my dad and a few of his friends had just returned from a trip to Iraq after they felt like God had called them there. He came back full of stories. But the ones that stood out to me were the ones about the Iraqi children.

I was in sixth grade at the time, at a Lebanese school in Beirut, and I wanted to do something for the children suffering in Iraq. The next day at school, I started brainstorming ideas with my best friend on ways we could help the kids in Iraq. We decided we would raise money in order to put together little bags filled with a few toys and basic necessities. We proceeded to design flyers and handmade magnets to hand out to classmates and teachers, asking for five hundred Lebanese lira—thirty cents.

I had always been a little shy in school, especially with my limited Arabic, so it was a good thing my Lebanese friend was a go-getter, convincing just about everyone to give away some of their change. We collected about sixty dollars, and we felt on top of the world with all that money. The best part was taking the money around the corner to the "500 Store" (the "30-Cent Store") and filling the bags with coloring books, crayons, socks, toothbrushes, and a few other items. We were able to fill up thirty bags.

Three weeks later, my dad and a few others returned to Iraq to hand out the bags and provide some other relief work. I wish I could have been there to personally deliver the bags to the Iraqi children.

A few days after we had sent the bags off, another friend, a few years younger, had heard about what my friend and I had done, so she decided to do the same thing and put together more bags for the children in Iraqi hospitals. It's crazy to see what happens when you choose to step out and do something that may seem intimidating or insignificant. But aren't we all just called to love? And in order to love, we're supposed to care. It seems second nature—there was a war going on in Iraq, and people needed care, so shouldn't we respond by caring for them? However, so often we miss those opportunities because we're too busy planning or over-analyzing. I know that I (now) miss it all the time. So next time an opportunity comes up, I hope I have the same spirit and mindset I had as a sixth-grader living in Lebanon.

Marie

Having lived in two very different "homes" has allowed me to have a broader view of the world and its differences. During those twelve years in Beirut, I felt content with where God had placed our family. I made numerous friends, mostly Muslim, which allowed me to break down prejudices that some of my American friends tend to have. A picture memory of Town Square, in downtown Beirut, remains in my mind: there were lights strung across the restaurant fronts, soothing Arabic music, the clanging of forks and knives, and people talking and laughing. Throughout my many evenings spent with my Arab friends, there was a strong sense of mutual understanding and community.

My life in Lebanon was completely different from my life here; I grew up knowing the life of the Lebanese, and I knew little about the American culture and their views on community and how they interacted with one another. I grew up fitting in with the Lebanese, not feeling at all out of place, even though I was the only American in my elementary school class. I even convinced myself that I was Lebanese. The number-one thing I learned from the Middle Eastern culture I grew up around was how to live in community. That key component held my life together, since I was surrounded by friends and people all the time, walking with me through life, making me who I am today. I often have flashbacks of times with my friends walking downtown late at night, laughing about how great life was and how we were so blessed to be a group of friends. When I think of these memories, I try to cover my sadness at leaving my friends behind with thoughts of how thankful I should be to have lived there at all. I made friends with all of my classmates in elementary school, but I held on to three of my best friends, with whom I still keep in touch and miss incredibly.

My American friends ask me why I get so excited when talking about Lebanon, eating Lebanese food, or meeting a Lebanese person. The reason is clear—it's because the friends I made and the experiences I remember have made a mark deep down in my heart. I simply have those "I miss Lebanon" days. I even met some Saudi Arabians on my college campus and I told them proudly that I had lived in Lebanon. They started talking to me in Arabic to test my comprehension of the language. I have lost a lot of my Arabic while being in America, but I could pick up a few words and could say a few phrases to them. That brought huge smiles to their faces as they told me I was the first American they'd met who knew some Arabic. I look forward to my life being continually surrounded by Arabs and Middle Easterners, as their culture has had so much influence on me and who I am. I am so grateful for my life and all God has given me.

Jon

Sometimes we're afraid because we don't understand or aren't familiar with other people and their culture. Not just a fear of being physically hurt, but a basic fear of simple communication.

I grew up in the Arab world. I was born in Damascus, Syria. Most of my friends were Arab Muslims. I spoke Arabic pretty fluently when I was little. I would correct my family if they said my friends' names with an American accent. For the most part, I thought I was Arab just like all my friends. I didn't know anything other than being Lebanese and speaking Arabic because that was the culture and people I was familiar with. The Middle East was my home.

When we moved to America, the most common question I got when I said I had lived in the Middle East was "Wow, did you feel afraid?" That question didn't make sense to me at the time. I didn't know if they were talking about the fast taxi drivers or the large cockroaches. But in my mind, the people were the last thing I was afraid of. I knew them only as friends and family.

When I was about nine years old, I was playing at a friend's house. He was one of my best friends in Lebanon, and he was a Muslim named Muhammad. We were just hanging out like usual, and then it was time for him to pray, and he asked me if I wanted to pray with him. I wasn't sure what that meant and was a little nervous to do it, but I ended up saying yes. I thought it would be cool. I mean, prayer is always good, right?

We washed our hands and arms before we started, and then he said, "Watch me, and follow what I do." I thought that was easy enough. But I asked, "What do I pray for or what do I say?" At this point, I was expecting him to explain the Muslim way of traditional prayer, but he responded, "Well, you know, the usual things, like asking for a GameCube." I think I was praying for that the past year anyway, so it was pretty easy.

I like this story because when we think of people as "different," whether it's cultural, religious, racial, or whatever, we forget that they are just like us with the same fears and hopes as we have.

By the way, I think Muhammad got a GameCube and I didn't. Not sure what that means, but just saying!

Love Like Dogs Love

One word frees us of all the weight and pain of life. That word is love.

Socrates

Love never fails.

The apostle Paul
to the Corinthians

Zoe is our family's nine-year-old golden retriever. I know it's not fair that our kids had to share a chapter while our dog gets a whole chapter, but she has a point to make. Plus, Zoe is amazing. Smart. Obedient. Personal. And everyone loves her.

I'll come back to my dog in a moment.

I've noticed an interesting phenomenon among some missionaries to Muslims in my over thirty years of working in that vineyard. It's sort of a self-fulfilling prophecy. With several variations, it goes something like this: Muslim soil is hard. By that I mean it takes years of building relationships with them before we can effectively share the good news of Jesus Christ. They are sometimes antagonistic to the gospel, and many of the countries where Muslims are the majority do not like us and what we do. The work of church planting is difficult, dangerous, and downright daunting (you might call them the three Ds of Muslim missions)!

Do you mind if I bring up a story I shared earlier in this book? It's when I went to Yemen as a twenty-year-old kid. You may recall that I spoke to the head of a large mission there who ran a hospital. A wonderful man. He and his wife were having their retirement party—going back to the United States after twenty-two years of faithful service. I was so excited to meet a real live missionary to Arab Muslims and so disappointed when he told me that in all that time, he had seen only two or three Yemenis come to the Lord. As wives sometimes do with us overexaggerating husbands, his wife even gently chided him: "Honey, I'd say one for sure and maybe two."

I tried to smile but couldn't. I didn't know what to say, or even what to think. They looked like they were okay with those numbers. I had been told—many times over—that Arab Muslims were "difficult" and not to expect too much fruit. So this seemed to simply confirm that teaching. Twenty-two years, and one, two, or maybe three Arab Muslims came to follow Jesus. There you have it. Teaching principle #1 confirmed.

I know the verses. They're in the Bible. The way is narrow. Like a camel going through the eye of a needle. The parable of the soil—only one in four seeds seems to make it. The odds are not in our favor. Few will be chosen. And it seems like Muslims are the fewest of the few. We have theology to back up our experience.

This task is difficult. Or is it?

Back to my golden retriever. It has to be at least a bit interesting to think for a moment about which comes first: most people liking my dog because my dog is inherently friendly—or my dog is so friendly because everyone likes her. Do you see the difference? Zoe has never met a "stranger." Everyone is her best friend. She never stops to think, *Hmmm, I wonder if that guy over there is a dog person.* Zoe thinks everyone is a dog person. She gets confused when someone doesn't lean over and pet her while making silly human noises.

So everyone likes Zoe. They tell us things like, "You have the nicest dog," or ask, "Are all golden retrievers this friendly?"

Yes, Zoe loves people. And people love her. But again, which came first? I think it's Zoe's assumption that every person in the world will love her—and then they do. It's like a self-fulfilling prophecy.

And that's what I think about Arab Muslims. I've met tens of thousands in my thirty-plus years of spending time in every Arabic-speaking nation. They all like me. From the Al Azhar University and Seminary in Cairo and the imams of Saudi Arabia, to the Hezbollah of southern Lebanon and the Hamas of Palestine, Arabs respond positively to me—and to our message of Jesus the Messiah. In every instance—100 percent of the time. Okay, one time a guy got angry at me. So 99.9 percent of the time. Why do you think this is?

It's because I assume Arab Muslims will like me. And more important, I assume they will want to hear the message of Jesus. And then they do. It is not because I'm so nice—or good-looking, suave, or debonair. Nope. It's just because I assume that Muslims will like me.

For every verse that sounds like Jesus is hard to get to and the path to him is narrow with tons of obstacles, I will show you five that are the opposite. They are inviting. Open. Easy. Remember James's end point in Acts 15:19? "We should not make it difficult for the Gentiles who are turning to God." Maybe *we* are the ones making it hard on Muslims to see and believe in and follow Jesus. They are not hard at all. They respond easily to Jesus.

The crowds loved Jesus. They followed him en masse. They wanted to make him king. Children came to him—and kids always know who's right on and who's messed up. Kids like only adults who like them. Same principle. And the kids and the poor and the sick—all those who had been disenfranchised by the system—came to Jesus. They sensed he was *for* them!

I have found that when I assume someone wants to know me and hear what I have to say, they do. This is not positive thinking on my part. It's not a method. It's faith working through love. Jesus loves ~~Muslims~~ people. I love what and who Jesus loves, so I love ~~Muslims~~ people. And when I love them, they love me back. We form bonds of trust. They give me access to their hearts, and I share with them the best news they'll ever hear.

It really is that simple. Perfect love casts out fear. And it can also be the other way around—fear can cast out love.

Let's be like Zoe.

Risky Hospitality

The Bible tells us to love our neighbors, and also to love our enemies; probably because generally they are the same people.

G. K. Chesterton

The King will reply, "Truly I tell you, whatever you did for one of the least of these brothers and sisters of mine, you did for me."

Jesus

*H*ospitality is derived from the Latin word *hospes,* which can mean either the "host" or the "visitor." And this word *hospes* is further derived from the Latin word *hostis,* which, quite interestingly, can mean a "stranger," a "foreigner," or an "enemy." The difference is a verb that has a friendly connotation and implies protection. From those two words respectively, we get *hospitality/hospitable/hospital* and *hostile/hostility.*

Do you want to know what's risky? I mean, like, really really risky? It's inviting your neighbors over for dinner. Think of what can go wrong:

- They just plain say no. How embarrassing is that?
- They come, but you realize you don't really like each other.

- You serve pork and wine to Muslims, and you didn't even know your neighbors were Muslim!
- Your gas grill runs out of propane halfway through cooking the burgers.
- You cook the burgers—till they're burned.
- You make everything just right, but you can tell the guests still don't like what you made.
- You ask fifty questions about them, and they ask exactly zero about you.
- You can tell you are their new best friend; they won't leave.
- Everything was planned for an evening outside, but it rains like crazy.
- They bring their little kids and expect your big kids to baby-sit.
- They bring their kids and, well, you wish they hadn't.

Other than that, nothing to worry about.

Now that I've basically talked you out of ever being hospitable to your neighbors, let me share some of our experiences.

First of all, I must say that both Chris and I come from very hospitable families. But Chris cheated: hers is Greek—enough said. Those warm-blooded Mediterranean types just seem to have a hospitality gene.

But somehow my parents were also incredibly hospitable, even though they're mostly Irish and German. So Chris and I have always valued hosting people and entertaining and making people feel at home—in our home. Unfortunately, that seems increasingly rare these days, especially here in the West.

So when we arrived in Beirut, we already "knew" hospitality. But then, well, we met Arabs. Wow! That's a whole new level of being kind, considerate, paying-the-bill-when-eating-out, inviting-you-in-even-when-you're-a-stranger, and generally being the nicest people on the planet. Okay, so we weren't all that hot after all. We were their hospitality apprentices.

But we learned. We took the leap and said yes to this new adventure. And as with all new adventures, not everything went that well.

I remember the time when we were serving dinner to a bunch of friends and making pizza from scratch (everything was from scratch, which was Big Problem #1; it didn't come in a box). Chris looked down at the pizza dough before she put it in the oven, and with her cute mouse-like squeaking noise, she called to me. "Carl, get in here. Something's wrong with the pizza dough."

I looked, and all I could see was white dough—with some added color. Little pink wiggly things. My response was, "Quick, bake it; they'll die and the guests will never know." (Last time you come to our house for dinner, eh?) Chris would have none of it, so we did what any normal American family would have done anyway—she sent me flying to the store to buy roasted chicken.

Then there's the time we served tacos to our neighbors who lived in the flat right below us. Hard-shelled tacos. You should have seen the looks on their faces when we put taco fixings in front of them with empty hard shells that surely looked to them like some inedible piece of cardboard. Ever try to convince someone that the food they're eating is good—even though they've never had it before? "Come on, guys. Tacos. Mexican food. An American favorite. You'll love it."

Naturally, Chris started cooking Lebanese food. Tabouli, hummus, fattoush, baba ghanouj, kibbe, shish tawouk, wara' einab (rolled grape leaves), and shawarma. You know—all that easy stuff.

The new challenge was that the Lebanese are serious food *connoisseurs*. No one is pickier than a Lebanese man who's used to exactly how his mother and his wife have made a dish for decades. And then along comes this silly American woman who tries to make it for the first time.

I used to host a weekly group of men at our house who were all Lebanese leaders. We were studying the life of Jesus together. It was awesome. I probably shouldn't say who they were exactly, but they were significant men in the public life of Beirut and Lebanon. One night during Ramadan, they all came to our house for Iftar. Iftar is the meal at the end of the day that breaks the day of fasting for a Muslim. All meals for Arabs are special, but this one, well, let's just say it has to be done just right. It has to be prepared perfectly. Served in exactly the correct fashion. And it better taste good—they're hungry.

Chris cooked the Iftar meal for ten Lebanese men. Wow, do I admire her. And do you know what—they loved it. Okay, that's not totally true. The mayor of West Beirut (oops, wasn't supposed to say that—I don't think he'll mind) did say, "This special Ramadan soup is too hot. It should be cooler!"

Everyone appreciated the effort. I doubt it tasted like their moms' home cooking, but it was edible, and Chris did it. I was so proud of her. That's a pretty big yes on her adventure. The boll weevils in the pizza dough, the hard tacos for our neighbors, and the many long hours of trying to make rolled stuffed grape leaves were paying off. She was learning the art of cooking. And not just any kind of cooking, but cooking from scratch, Lebanese style. That's risky hospitality!

We quickly learned that the way Arabs give hospitality is the way they expect it. Sometimes whole families would show up at our flat at nine or even ten at night, and we had to be ready.

Showing up unannounced at someone's house has its own word in Arabic. Translated into English it's just the word *visiting*, which is used like a noun. What they'd do for us if we showed up at their house was amazing. They'd usually call out the whole family—there was no such thing as the kids staying in their rooms. Everyone came out and said hello and sat with us for at least a little while before returning to whatever they had been doing earlier.

Then they'd bring out the food. No matter what the time. At the least there would be nuts, fruit, cookies, and whatever they'd had for dinner (of course there were leftovers, because they always cooked enough to serve all of Beirut, in case all of Beirut showed up that night). Then they'd peel the oranges or kiwis, cut up the apples for us, and hand them to us ready to eat, and then bring in a whole tray of drinks. Hot and cold drinks. Juice. Lemonade. Soda. Water. Tea and coffee. And we would chat. And eat. And eat and chat. And they would never think of suggesting that it was getting late and we might want to head home. In fact, whenever we would get ready to leave, someone would inevitably say, "What, so early?" Or fairly often they would invite us to spend the night. I don't think they really thought we'd spend the night, but we sure could have if we'd wanted to.

What's crazy-amazing about this is that we could be walking through a village outside of Beirut where no one knew us, and all of the above could happen. We'd get invited in, have dinner, and then they'd insist we spend the night. And sometimes we did. It's a great way to make new friends!

Our neighbors rescued us far more often than we did anything for them. There were times when Chris was home alone (remember, I was out saving the world), and neighbors would bring food to the door.

We would be so exhausted sometimes from life being so busy and trying to live in another culture that when people would show up unannounced at our door—especially if it was late in the evening—we would just hide behind the couch and wait till they left. How's that for a confession? Yep, we'd hide from the people we came to serve and love and show the way of Jesus. What's worse, our kids would hide with us—they thought it was a fun game.

There's an Arabic word that when transliterated sounds like *t'fadoul*. It's what you say when someone shows up, and it loosely means "we'd love for you to come in."

So we made up our own word for when people would show up at our house—we called them the *t'fadoulers*. I can't tell you how many times we'd be nestled in our castle (you know, your home is your castle?), and the kids were finally asleep; it was 9:30, we were exhausted, and the doorbell would ring. Seldom, if ever, did we say, "Oh, praise the Lord, more people." It was more like, "Great, we have *t'fadoulers* at our door." Usually we'd suck it up, put on a big smile, and welcome them with food, drinks, and open arms. And imagine this—many of those times ended up being the sweetest times we ever had.

But sometimes, we'd hide behind the sofa.

Finally, though, saying yes to this risky adventure called hospitality started to pay off. Despite our mistakes, we started to get it.

Think about it—God has shown us the ultimate hospitality, and he also asks us to be hospitable to him by serving others.

Jesus served his disciples, even washing their feet (when they should have washed his). He showed us how to treat traitors and enemies when he washed Judas's feet. Can you imagine? He knew Judas would betray him and yet he washed his feet. That's hospitality.

Jesus entered our world and took the risk of the ultimate act of hospitality by becoming one of us. To live like we live, feel what we feel, breathe and eat and drink and laugh and cry like we do. Jesus sets the standard. That's what true hospitality is—knowing what the other would want in order to feel comfortable and at home, and then providing it.

And Jesus also asks it of us, toward him.

He stands at the door and knocks. Will we let him in?

As many as received him, he gave the power to be the sons of God. Do we receive him or hide behind the sofa? (Ouch.)

Even the metaphors so often used in the Gospels of Jesus being the bread, water, salt, and light can all be read through the lens of good hospitality. It's serving others—not focusing on our immediate needs, but those of our guests. Jesus was the ultimate giver of good hospitality, and he asks the same of us.

Our beautiful Lebanese hosts showed us this side of Jesus. Even through the war years, they would visit each other, cook huge meals, laugh and play cards, and continue with living. Perhaps this was the secret to their survival. While many of us in the Western world have withdrawn into our private lives, with our homes increasingly being our own private spaces, the Eastern world still takes seriously the art of visiting their neighbors. Though their lives seem much worse than ours, depression and suicide are largely Western issues. Loneliness may be the bane of our age in the Western world.

But we can change that. We must stir up the gift of hospitality that God has placed in each one of us.

Part of being a good host is being prepared. We learned to have stacks of nuts, chips, drinks, and all kinds of goodies on hand at all times. That sounds so simple, but it wasn't easy to learn for some reason. We were seldom surprised when people showed up.

We learned to cook *far* more than was needed. Both Chris and I come from the Midwest, where the highest value on cooking seems to be making exactly the right amount of food—not a ladle more. Not sure where that comes from, but I can remember taking great pride in having exactly the right amount for our needs.

But having extra seems to be a value of Jesus. There are many stories of his extravagance, but my favorite is the wedding at Cana. Most biblical scholars agree that the jars of water he turned into wine would have been equivalent to about nine hundred bottles. *What?* Who needs nine hundred bottles of wine—at the end of the party? Answer: no one. But Jesus did it anyway. Why? Real answer is—I have no idea. But the answer I like, because it fits what I'm writing about, is that Jesus is extravagant. He's generous. He likes to go over the top. Above and beyond.

Last week Chris and I had dinner at the home of our friends Greg and June. They made way too much food. We had various appetizers, then chicken and salad, and the burgers hadn't even come yet. We had several kinds of drinks and then dessert. Way, way too much. The funny thing is that we all complained about having too much food and being "so full I can hardly move," and all that stuff we say when we're being fed like cattle going to slaughter. But do you know what? We loved every minute of it. We felt doted upon. Taken care of. Loved. Something about having too much is a good thing.

I know, I know. There's the possibility someone will bring up the book *Rich Christians in an Age of Hunger,* and say that we all have too much and should share our food with the rest of the world—which would be good hospitality. I totally agree. But this isn't about that—that's another point (and a good one). This is about being generous with what we do have with the people around us (wherever we live) who are lost, lonely, and in need of food, spiritual and otherwise.

And don't miss one of the main points about the power of hospitality: Good food and friendship and drink and conversation open hearts to God. Do you know how many times food, drink, and meals are referenced in the Bible? Hundreds. Jesus clearly knew the importance of a well-cooked meal. John 21 chronicles one of these great stories about Jesus and food.

Some of the disciples had gone back to fishing. We don't know why they'd taken it up again, but there they were. Turns out Jesus had been on the shore cooking breakfast. We assume he was cooking enough for those in the boat—not just for himself—since he invited them to eat with him.

Anyway, he called out, asking if they'd caught any fish. They hadn't. So he told them to throw their net on the other side of the boat. Several things are funny here. Among them is the fact that they didn't even know it was Jesus calling to them, yet they did what he said anyway. Another thing I don't understand is why in the world, after fishing all night, they would cast their net on the other side of the boat—as if the fish would be over there and not where they'd been?

But they did, and John records that they hauled in 153 large fish. Did you get that? Sort of like the water-into-wine story. *One hundred fifty-three fish.* And John is careful to note that they were large fish.

Finally, once again, Peter jumped into the water to get to Jesus. He could have waited a few minutes to get to shore, but he was anxious to get to Jesus, impetuous as usual.

All sounds extravagant to me. Almost careless and reckless. Irresponsible. But then there's the nine hundred bottles of wine, walking on water, pouring out expensive perfume to anoint Jesus, listening at his feet rather than cooking dinner, feeding five thousand people fish and chips for lunch—all a bit much. I'd have been a bit more conservative and a lot less wasteful.

But Jesus was concerned about food and drink and ambiance. He knew its power.*

Back to Chris and me. The point I want to make is that we did learn hospitality. We learned from our Lebanese neighbors. Then we started seeing it everywhere in the Scriptures. Is it like that for you? First you start to see or experience something, and then, only then, do you see it in the Bible. Sort of like buying a new car and suddenly realizing everyone else drives that same car.

Once, at Easter, Chris and I decided to invite some of the leaders of a large Bedouin tribe to our house for lunch. We should have known. By inviting their families, it could have been several hundred people. They were gracious to us—they must have known we couldn't have handled that—so only about twenty came. But this time, we were ready. Chris cooked an amazingly yummy and huge meal. They spent the whole day at our house. Our kids did an Easter egg hunt with their kids. (I know, Easter and bunnies and hiding eggs don't go together. It's a pagan practice, and—I know, I know. But they all had a lot of fun!)

The Jesus conversations we had that day were amazing. And the long-term doors that opened with this community of Muslim Bedouins are partially a testament to good hospitality.

---

*My friend Conrad Gempf wrote an excellent book on this topic called *Mealtime Habits of the Messiah*. A very good read.

Earlier I mentioned our little student-and-community center called the Olive Grove. During the fasting month of Ramadan, some of our college students had the idea to serve the Iftar meal at the Olive Grove for the poor. We didn't really know if it would work or how many would come. But, you guessed it—we did it anyway.

And about fifty came the first night. All of our students (and our family) had worked all day cooking and preparing. It was fun for many reasons, but one of the main ones was that some of our young people were from Christian backgrounds and didn't really even know what an Iftar was all about or what kind of food should be made or how it should be served. They learned a lot about their neighbors.

We all liked doing it so much we decided to do an Iftar meal every Tuesday night through the month of Ramadan. The place was packed. I think we had a hundred people there the last night. And one of the Lebanese members of Parliament came that night—everyone was so excited. Most of these poor people had never meant an MP before, and now he was eating with them.

Let me say one final thing about good hospitality. It's not about setting people up for a good sermon. You don't feed people and make them feel comfortable so that you can "get them." You do it out of a generous spirit that reflects God's love for us that "while we were yet sinners. . . ." We provide a hospital (hospitality) for hurting, lonely souls because that was once us.

Hospitality is just being a good human being. And yes, in the midst of sharing food and conversation, people's hearts and minds do open up to other things that are good news. Namely a person: Jesus.

From Christianity
to Christ to Jesus—
My Fears of (Not)
Being Right

I believe in getting into hot water; it keeps you clean.

G. K. Chesterton

For now we see only a reflection as in a mirror; then we shall see face to face. Now I know in part; then I shall know fully, even as I am fully known.

The apostle Paul to the Corinthians

One of my innermost secret fears is that of being wrong. Some might call that pride. I like to call it "I don't like being wrong because I love the truth."

All my life I've studied the Scriptures. I was that weird kid in junior high who took his Bible with him to school and had a "One Way" button on his shirt. I had "Jesus Saves" stickers, and I invited kids to Wednesday night youth group. I was on the Colorado Springs Bible trivia team, and I always beat everyone else at sword drills (you know, when someone says a verse and you all race to find it first). Yep, that was me. I knew the Bible, and I knew theology.

In my late teens and twenties, I read and loved Athanasius, Aquinas, Anselm, Augustine, and other deceased Catholic scholars starting with the letter *A*.

I read classic works: Calvin's *Institutes*; the writings of Martin Luther, Zwingli, and Knox. I knew the early church fathers—those who lived in the deserts of Egypt and amazing guys like John of the Cross, Justin Martyr, Origin, and Tertullian. When I was younger, I read Jerome and Eusebius and actually did my college senior thesis paper on the Council of Nicea and the debate between Arius and Athanasius about the nature of Jesus.

I loved (and still love) good doctrine and a good debate. I taught an adult Sunday school class when I was nineteen on J. I. Packer's book *Knowing God* and loved it (probably way more than those poor souls who had to sit and listen to a punk kid rambling on about how much theology he knew—almost as much as Packer himself).

But part of this obsession with the Bible and theology and Christian history was so that I would always know more than the next guy. He would have no chance of beating me at this game. In particular, no one else my age could know more than me, yet I found that even most adults didn't know any more. And let me say that it wasn't all driven out of some weird place in my heart to always be right—not all of it. I did love God, and I wanted nothing more than to follow Jesus and do what was right. But much of it came from some place of insecurity, some place of fear. (Have I mentioned yet that fear and insecurity and pride and worry are all actually the same thing?)

Okay, so maybe I can't just drop that one-liner in parentheses and move on. So here's a little more on that statement.

When I look at my life and what has scared me in the past or scares me now, it could be called "pride" or "insecurity." Either one. Both are focused on self.

What makes me insecure? It could be as simple as thinking someone is looking at me weird. Or that I might say the wrong thing. Or that someone doesn't respect me as I think they should. Isn't that pride? And aren't both pride and insecurity types of fear? I think so.

Funny thing is, just tonight (as I'm writing this) I had such a moment. I had given one of my books, *Speaking of Jesus*, to my neighbor. She and her husband call themselves atheists. Chris and I have talked with them a lot. They've been in our home many times; they come every year to our Christmas party. And we've shared much of what we believe and why. We are friends; we really know them.

About a month ago, I gave them my book. After that, every time I saw them, I wanted to ask if they'd read it, but I just couldn't bring myself to ask. Why is that? Insecurity, right? There are only so many possible answers to the question "Have you read my book?"

1. "Yes, and I loved it."
2. "No, we haven't."
3. "Yes, and we didn't like it."

You might notice that two of those three answers would make me feel bad. So—I never asked.

Until tonight. The wife told me, "Oh, actually our eleven-year-old picked it up, and he's reading it. He seems to like it because he won't give it back."

What? Whew.

So what was my insecurity? It was really pride. Good old-fashioned pride. I wanted to look good but was afraid I wouldn't. Insecurity is just pride in another form.

That's the Carl who moved to Beirut in 1992 as a thirty-year-old know-it-all. And boy, did I ever know Christianity. Its reasons. Its doctrines. Its theologies. I knew Finney and Wesley and Edwards inside and out. I had grown up in an Arminian home and had then moved to more of a Calvinistic position, but after much study, I was now perfectly situated in the middle of those two—where all thinking Christians should be, right? Some of both sides had good points, and I was comfortable in the middle.

By the time we arrived in Beirut, I was probably voted "Most Likely to Be an Amazing Missionary to Muslims" by almost everyone I knew. My church. My denomination. My mission agency. My friends and family. And of course, me. We all thought I would be awesome. And do you know what? I actually was pretty good at being a Christian missionary. I've already written some on this, so I'll get right down to it . . .

Christianity. The word is not in the Bible. Actually, a really funny thing is that the word *Bible* also isn't in the Bible. *Missionary* isn't. *Church planting* isn't there. *Evangelism*—nope. *Senior pastor.* You get the idea.

I've written and spoken on these things a lot, and the first reaction when I say any of this is that I'm being silly with my semantics, and while those words may not be in the Scriptures (notice, I didn't say "Bible"), we know that the concepts are. So then why does it matter what you call them?

Remember, this is a book about fear—overcoming or working through it. And right here is where my two greatest fears collide: pleasing people and being right. Those two don't work that well together. On the one hand, I want to be right theologically—know the Scriptures better than you—and on the other hand, I want and need people to like me. I'm a classic people-pleaser. The challenge, of course, is that no one likes a know-it-all.

People generally don't like it when you suggest that all they've believed and much of what they've done—and how they've done it—may not be the best way. *Speaking of Jesus* is a whole book on why I don't believe in evangelism (the book's subtitle is *The Art of NOT-Evangelism*). Not everyone caught the vision of Jesus' words to "make disciples," and that the thing we call "evangelism" actually doesn't exist in the Scriptures. Then people get mad at me, and I want to explain myself until they understand, because I don't want them to feel bad. Mostly, I don't want them to be angry at me because it makes *me* feel bad.

And around and around we go. Unless I'm secure.

Ever notice how secure Jesus was in his identity? He didn't have to be. He could have wondered out loud about this whole incarnation thing and whether he really was God in the flesh or just a uniquely gifted Joe.

He was fully human in every way. We are all insecure. Why wasn't he?

Remember the passage in John 6, when he tells the disciples that if they want to have eternal life they must eat his flesh and drink his blood? A bunch of them were disgusted (rightly so, I'd say) and left him. Did you get that? Not just the crowds, but some of his closest followers and friends. And it says that "many" of them left.

Now think about this for a moment. You've given your whole life to these men and women, and you say one slightly confusing thing and they stop hanging out with you. What would you do? I'll tell you what I'd do—I'd explain myself. If I were Jesus, I'd have told them that I didn't really mean to literally eat my body and drink my blood—that'd be cannibalism. "That's disgusting. Come back here. I can explain . . ." That's what I would've said and done.

Not Jesus. He turned to the twelve confused but still committed disciples and asked if they wanted to leave as well. Wow.

I would never have done that. "I offended you? So do you want to leave?" Nope—wouldn't have done it.

Now, let's be clear on this—he's Jesus. His motives are pure. He wasn't being a jerk. Not acting cocky or arrogant. He was speaking truth. So I don't have a hall pass to go around saying offensive things, and then when people get mad to just say "too bad." Oh, believe me, I've done that. And I kind of like it. The only problem is, I'm not Jesus, so I can't get away with that.

But sometimes, just sometimes, I am saying something that's hard to hear and is actually true. And when people get offended or freak out and write nasty things about me, I need to be secure. Not afraid. To walk in faith in what I know to be true and let the chips fall where they fall.

One of those life-shaping moments for me was in 1993 (our early years) in southern Lebanon. I'd been asked to speak in a mosque. To preach, basically, by the imam. Pretty amazing opportunity, and, as you might imagine, I was scared to death.

As I walked up the stairs to the platform to address about two hundred Shi'ite Muslim men, the imam ran up behind me and tapped me on the shoulder. "Mr. Carl, Mr. Carl," he said. "One thing. Please don't speak about Christianity, just Jesus." And then he sat down in the front row.

Stunned and slightly confused as to what he meant, I turned and began to speak—about Jesus.

Of course, I was already going to talk about Jesus. But the imam's words and the way he emphasized "just Jesus" rang in my ears as I spoke.

They had given me forty-five minutes to talk. I spoke about what Jesus said, what he did, and a couple of his parables. It was pretty good. At the end of my time, the imam gave me the winding finger sign—you know, to keep going. I panicked; I'd given it my all. How much more could I say and stay on topic—Jesus?

Here I was, a Christian missionary—a full-time professional—and all I had was forty-five minutes on Jesus. I stumbled through another forty-five minutes, but I left that night a changed man. I realized I was missing one thing—the same things the Pharisees had missed: Jesus. I had Christianity. Church. Doctrine and theology. The Bible.

I had somehow missed Jesus.

And that set me on a journey that I'm still on now. To know Jesus. Actually know him. To love him. Worship him. Follow him. Believe in him. Believe what he believes and know what he knows. To love the Father the way he did. To honor the things and the ones he honors.

But to be totally honest, my first reaction was one of methodology—missiology. My thought was this: I needed to be better at presenting Christ, not Christianity, to Muslims because they were offended by Christianity (for tons of reasons) but seemed to like Christ.

So I would say I moved from preaching Christianity to preaching Christ. Not a bad move. But it still wasn't Jesus. Huh? What's the difference, you say? Glad you asked; let me explain.

First of all, my fears were still getting the best of me. I was afraid of being irrelevant. Of being a failure. I wanted Muslims to know Jesus, for sure, but I also didn't want to fail. Those two motives were mixed in my head and heart in such a way that I could hardly discern which was which. I had received a revelation to my brain that Muslims don't appreciate Christian stuff, because of the Crusades and the way they perceive the

West, etc. So I should stop saying "Christian" things. I even stopped calling myself a Christian at that point. I was now a "follower of Christ." Sounded much better and everyone seemed happy, which was good because I wanted people to be happy.

Okay, this is a little heavy, but follow along for a minute. Jesus was mostly referred to as Jesus in the Gospels. That's his name. Not his title, but his name. Really, it would have been Joshua—*Yeshua* in Hebrew or *Yesu* in Aramaic. But basically a version of Joshua. Josh. A very common name. That's his name. In English we say Jesus. In Arabic he has two names, either *Isa* (if you're Muslim) or *Yesua* (if you're a Christian Arab). All those names refer to the same historical man born in Bethlehem and raised in Nazareth.

So when Jesus was physically with us on earth, people called him by his name, as you'd expect. After he was crucified, rose again, and ascended to the Father, Paul and the other writers of Scripture still called him Jesus sometimes, but more and more referred to him by his various titles: Christ, Lord, Lord Jesus Christ, and others like Son of God or the Word. They are, in fact, his titles. They describe him, but they are not his name.

Chris is my wife. But I do not go around calling her "Wife." She wouldn't appreciate that, not because she doesn't like being my wife (you can ask her about that another time), but because her name is Chris. It's true that one of her many titles is wife, but it's not very personal or endearing if I call her by that title.

Do you get where I'm headed with this? (Just say "Yes, Carl, we get it.") Referring to Jesus as the Lord or as Christ isn't wrong or bad; it's just not very intimate. He is the Lord and the Christ (the Anointed One—the King). He is and he will always be. And we want our friends to see that in Jesus. But I believe that introducing Jesus first as our friend and brother is actually more effective and in some ways actually has more integrity. Because while we know that he is the King of the world, the one we're speaking to may not know that. So we set the bar low. Then Jesus, the person, can invite that friend in front of us, who doesn't yet know him, into his presence. One step at a time.

But really, the bigger issue was me—I didn't know Jesus. I didn't know his ways. His teachings. His life. I had never seriously considered why he spoke in parables. I didn't even know the parables.

Can we take a quick interlude here to talk about the parables for a second?

Imagine that you are God. Don't get too carried away with that, but just for a second. And you're hanging out one day at home in heaven, thinking about the best strategy to communicate with humans, when you send Jesus down to talk to them and explain some things. And you come up with this: "Hey, I know," the Father says to the Son, "how about if you tell them about forty-five very short stories that make absolutely no sense at all, and when they ask you to explain them—you don't?"

"Got it," says Jesus. And that's what he did.

Seriously, have you thought deeply about this? It's true. Once, when the twelve knuckleheads asked Jesus what he was talking about, he even said, "I speak this way [in riddles] so people won't understand, because if they did, they would repent." Well, there you have it.

We've come up with some great three- and four-point sermons for most of the parables, but really, if we deal with them honestly, they are pretty disturbing little vignettes of information.

Or what about this one? Why did Jesus so seldom answer the question he was asked? He never answered trick questions, but he also seemed to have an aversion to answering anyone directly. He'd ask them a question back, tell a story that seemingly had nothing to do with the question asked, or just not answer at all.

I've been taught to have an answer for every question. Not Jesus. And I've learned that whenever I find myself always doing what Jesus never did, I should stop doing that! Why do I feel the need to answer every question? Who said I should do that? The Scriptures don't tell me to answer everyone's questions about everything. Maybe it's because I'm insecure; I want people to know that I know the answer. Or I don't like being wrong or misunderstood, so I explain myself. Jesus didn't do that. Never. So stop it.

Okay, back to our original programming. What was I saying before I went on that little Jesus rant? Oh yeah, about how I had strategically moved from Christianity to Christ, but still needed to take one more step to Jesus. This is a huge point, if you can catch it. It will bring a ton of freedom to how you relate to Jesus and how you help the world see him.

You see, as I've let go of my need to always be right and instead focus on knowing Jesus more intimately and his ways more carefully, I've been more secure in who I am and how I present him. This does not mean I think we should be sloppy about our doctrine. Not at all. I want to know and love the Jesus who actually is—not the one I've made up in my head. I've just realized it's been my own fears that insist I always know the answers. That has been a security blanket for me. When I admit it, I realize that Jesus is so big that he confuses me. He calls me, but I don't see him and don't know where he's going. This means I have to jump in and trust him; I have to say yes to the next thing in front of me. I see through a glass darkly, but I do see just enough to say yes.

It's Peter peering at Jesus through the dense fog on a rainy, windy night. "Is that you, Lord?" Peter asks. "If it is, call me to come and I'll jump out of the boat and come." And Jesus says, "Come." And we do.

We say yes because it's Jesus calling.

Failure Is an Option

I've missed more than 9,000 shots in my career. I've lost almost 300 games. Twenty-six times I've been trusted to take the game-winning shot and missed. I've failed over and over and over again in my life. And that is why I succeed.

Michael Jordan

Let us not become weary in doing good, for at the proper time we will reap a harvest if we do not give up.

The apostle Paul to the Galatians

I can't tell you how many times I've messed something up. Thought something was "from God," and maybe it was and I just screwed it up all by myself, or it wasn't and it never had a chance. Just now—like, right now—I tried counting all the things I've started or tried to start over the years that I thought were from God but didn't work. But I gave up after about ten minutes, partly because there were too many to count and partly because it was depressing. I've failed a lot.

Failure's an interesting thing, isn't it? Most of us are afraid to fail, which makes it seem like a rational fear. After all, who wants to fail? Yet most of us fail most of the time in life. Think about all the guys or girls you dated before you met the right one. In a sense, those were failures. Or how many tests you took that you didn't get an A on. Or how many baskets or nets you missed when you took that shot. The best baseball players in the world fail to get on base the vast majority of the time. Think of the jobs you've had or the financial hardships and fix-it projects around the house you've attempted.

Failure is part of everyday life, but we act like it isn't there. So how do you think about that—if, in fact, you let yourself think about it at all?

I've read that 80 to 85 percent of all businesses started in America fail. That's in a country that at least theoretically encourages entrepreneurship. Of all the really bright gifted men and women in the land of opportunity, most fail to succeed. You might say that the most important decision you make in your life is whom you marry. About 50 percent of marriages don't work out. We try to lose weight but can't. We make New Year's resolutions we don't keep. We attempt to impress someone and it backfires.

And still we pretend we're not failures. Now, I'm going to ruffle some feathers with this one. I know we are all fond of saying things like, "I may fail, but I'm not a failure." Nice try.

What do we call someone who sails? A sailor. What about someone who drinks alcohol too much? An alcoholic. What about a person who gambles regularly? A gambler. Or to be more positive—what about someone who loves to shepherd people? A pastor (shepherd). The action when done consistently does become the noun. That's how language works.

I know we're trying to be positive and to see ourselves as God sees us. But I don't mind saying that for someone who has failed as much as I have, I could be called a failure. I'm pretty sure that's part of what redemption's for. It's good news that Jesus came for failures. It's the sick who need a doctor, not the healthy. And so here I am, in need of someone to rescue me. I need saving.

If we're going to fail, and even be "failures," we might as well go big. Let's attempt something so great for God that unless he's in it, it's doomed for failure. The rub comes when we think we are doing just that—and it still falls flat. What then?

Story time. About three years ago, I was on a trip with some guys from the States to visit Lebanon, Jordan, Palestine, and Israel. Because of jet lag, I woke up at four in the morning and decided to go out for a walk. We were staying near the most prestigious five-star hotel in Beirut, and as I walked by, I saw soldiers everywhere setting up roadblocks and looking around suspiciously.

It was then I remembered that the then-president of Iran, Mahmoud Ahmadinejad, was supposed to be in town that day or the next. So I had a thought. Ready? Here's my whole thought: *Boy, would I love to meet the president and talk to him about Jesus.*

So with that clear plan of action, I started walking toward the hotel and the checkpoint closest to me. When I got within fifty yards, the one soldier was joined by two others. They nervously faced me as I walked up to them and said, *"Sabah il Kheir"* (Good morning). They sort of just stared at me like, *Who is this weird white guy trying to speak Arabic at 4:15 in the morning at our checkpoint?*

I switched to English—as if they'd know it—and just blurted out, "Hey, I'm going to the hotel. Do you mind if I pass?"

"Where are you from?" one of the soldiers asked.

"America."

Apparently not impressed, he answered, "Well, you can't go to the hotel unless you're staying there."

I wasn't.

"Okay, so it's okay if I pass?"

The soldiers looked at each other a little confused and said, "Sure. Have a nice day."

My heart was pounding as I walked past them and into the hotel. *Is the president really here? What in the world am I doing?* I had no idea. So I walked up to the front desk and said, "Hi. My name is Carl Medearis, and I'd like to have a word with President Ahmadinejad."

"Uh, what?" said the startled desk jockey. "Do you have an appointment with the president?"

"Oh, so he's here now? Yes, I'd like to speak with him."

"Yes, but do you have an appointment?" (Remember, it's about 4:30 in the morning; who would have an appointment with a president at that time anyway?) Hilarious.

"I don't have one, but I'm sure if he knew what we were going to talk about, he'd want to talk to me," I said with feigned confidence.

"Really, and what is that you are going to talk to him about?" asked the desk clerk.

"Jesus," I responded with actual confidence now. *Of course that's what we'd talk about, and of course he'd want to talk about that.*

"One minute," said the guy, who then disappeared into the back after asking me to "have a seat over there."

About three minutes later, two guys with black leather jackets and sunglasses (I'm not making this up) walked up to me and shook my hand as I stood up. They looked at the piece of paper where I'd scribbled my name (I don't have a business card) and called me "Mr. Med-ear-eees."

"Yes," I answered. "And who are you?"

"We are in charge of the president's security detail," one of them said in perfect English.

Ah, so he is here. I was getting excited.

They asked if I had an appointment, and I said, "No, but I'd sure like one."

They asked why, and I said this: "I know that your president has a special place in his heart for Jesus Christ. I am an expert on the ways and life of Jesus, and I would like to discuss this with your president."

They looked only slightly shocked, as if someone had announced a deep secret but they already knew what it was. They immediately leaned toward me. "Yes, you're right. He loves the Messiah. And I'm sure he'd want to talk about that, but he's sleeping right now and then has a very busy day. Could you perhaps meet with him in two days, just before he leaves?"

My heart jumped out of my chest with excitement but landed again firmly where it's supposed to be when I realized we would be flying to Jordan the morning after next. I pleaded for time that very day, but there was none.

We talked for a while and I left, disappointed. I'd failed. But it sure was fun. I waved at the soldiers as I passed their curious looks on the way out. All that, and it was still only five in the morning.

My friends and I had a full day planned. Every hour was taken with people we were meeting. Around midday, we headed to the south of Lebanon to meet with the number-two guy in the Hezbollah, sheikh Nabeel Qawook. I've written extensively about him in my coauthored book with Ted Dekker, *Tea with Hezbollah*.

When we entered the sheikh's house, one of the first things he said was, "Hey, Carl, guess who's coming down here today?"

"Who?"

"President Ahmadinejad will be here in about three hours to spend the rest of the day with me."

What?

One problem: In three hours my friends and I had to be back in Beirut for a meeting with a member of Parliament that couldn't be changed or canceled. *So close.* Still, in our time with the Hezbollah leader, he talked about the difficulty of following the command of Jesus to love our enemies (something I've frequently challenged the sheikh to do). After an hour or so, we all gathered around him, laid hands on him, and prayed in the name of the one who gave that command. As always, the sheikh loved it. We hugged and kissed and said good-bye.

We drove back north as the president of Iran flew in a helicopter in the opposite direction.

I was zero for two. Three's a strikeout.

That evening, my Lebanese friend who was hosting us got a phone call from the Hezbollah leader we had seen that morning. The sheikh was all excited. "Tell Mr. Carl that I talked for a long time with Ahmadinejad about Mr. Carl and what he does and talks about. And he was really excited and wants to meet tomorrow."

Of course, we had to leave Lebanon that next day.

But after learning about our plans, the Hezbollah leader called back later that night and said, "I spoke some more with the president, and he would like to host Mr. Carl and a delegation of Christian leaders in Iran to talk about 'the Christ and the end times.'" (Those were his actual words.)

Eh? Guess I'd need to read the Left Behind series after all. I was a little fuzzy on my charts, but I guess I could brush up. *The end times? What on earth is going on?*

"Tell him yes," I said. Yes. Yes. Yes.

I flew home to the States and worked for about three months on a return trip to Iran. I brought together an amazing group of the top Christian leaders in America. Ten names I'm sure you'd know. Kudos to them for agreeing to head off to Iran with me to meet President Ahmadinejad to talk about "the Christ and the end times." He had promised us two full days of his time. Then we would speak at some universities and have other meetings around the country. We'd be in Iran for about one week total. It was a dream.

This was happening at the end of January 2011. The Arab Spring had entered into a new and serious phase in Cairo on January 25 of that year. We bought our plane tickets on February 1. By then massive protests were breaking out all over the Middle East and there was chaos on the streets of Tehran.

I received an email from the Iranian president's office saying we needed to "indefinitely postpone" our meeting. Within an hour of getting our tickets, the whole trip was canceled. I felt sick.

Strike three.

That trip still has never happened. All the relational equity I spent convincing these high-level Christian leaders in America that this was the real deal and not some fly-by-night fantasy of a crazy guy named Carl and the nutty president of Iran was, well, all out the window. I looked the fool, and once again, my insecurity about looking stupid and not being able to please these men whom I admire greatly reared its ugly head. What was I thinking? How could I have been so naïve as to think I could pull this off?

Yes, plenty of friends counseled me not to feel bad. "I'm sure something good came out of it," some said. Others quoted our favorite verse for confusing times: "In all things God works for the good . . . " (Romans 8:28).

Yeah, whatever!

All I know is that the trip didn't work. I was gravely disappointed and confused. It seemed "so God." How could it not happen? It was the perfect lesson. I had tried out of my own strength (brashly going to the hotel in the middle of the night), only to have God do it without my help through the Hezbollah leader later that same day. Isn't that how God works? Of course it is.

I know how God works: I try my best and then he shows up! Then I get on board with him—and then it works. Wham! No? Well, I guess not. At least not this time. I felt like a failure. Okay, just so I don't totally lose some of you, I'll stop saying I'm a failure. I simply failed. What? You don't even like that? I know that you want me to say something like "I was faithful. I tried my best. Cast your bread on the waters. Leave the results to him." Those sorts of things that make us feel better—and might actually be true, as well.

But let's think about why we say those things. Really, why do we go through all of that theologizing? What if, instead, we were just okay with something not working? We try something, it doesn't work out, and we're okay with it; we move on. That actually feels to me like it has more integrity.

We don't know why all the time—even most of the time. If the results really are up to God, then why should we feel compelled to explain them? What if we actually "let go and let God"? Relaxed a bit when it comes to things not working out and our spending hours and days trying to understand why. Since I'm pretty sure we're never going to know the answer to most of these whys anyway, let's just chill a bit, get up, shake off our boots, and move on.

I had an adventure in the process, that's for sure. Loved the whole thing, except the not-working part. Talk about an adventure in saying yes!

Can I encourage you a bit? Don't be afraid to fail. It's one of our biggest fears. You are going to fail. Period. If you try anything, you'll likely fall down.

You know there is an answer to failure. It's not giving up.
Don't give up. You will reap a harvest, in the right time, if you
do not give up.

Fail on! Just don't quit.

The Medearis family was sitting at our dinner table one
night in our cozy home on our cul-de-sac in an idyllic suburb
of Denver, with our golden retriever at our side, when our
oldest, Anna, had a question.

"Shouldn't we do something about the Israeli-Palestinian
thing?"

*Really? I mean, if there's anyone who wants to do something
about "that thing," surely it's me.*

"Like what?" I asked back.

"Well, you know, maybe we can make a movie or something
that would highlight the issues so people in America would
understand more."

That was Anna's answer: a movie.

So, I've been sort of selling myself to you, the reader, as
Mr. Faith. Huge vision, big picture, you-can-do-anything faith
guy. Except this was, well, I don't really know—different.
First of all, it was my nineteen-year-old daughter. Second,
neither she, nor we, had ever made a movie, and none of us
were particularly good at even taking basic still photos. Other
than that . . .

"Sure, honey"—is what came out of my mouth—"of course
we can do that. What would be the next steps?"

"Well, I've been thinking that maybe my friend Joe, who is
a budding videographer, might come with us."

"Us?"

168

"Yeah, maybe we could go to Israel and Palestine as a family, like this coming summer or something," she said with not too much confidence.

Kids. *Like we could really just pack up, fly our family of five plus Joe to the Middle East to do a film that we don't know how to make. Where does she think we'll get the money?*

So we did it.

Anna and her nineteen-year-old high school friend Joe made a documentary. Marie did some artwork for it. Jon held the second camera and lugged stuff around. (I found out that person is called a key grip—who knows why?)

It was what people in the business call "a short," not a full-length film. Twenty-two minutes to be exact. And it was good. We spent two weeks running all over the Holy Land, interviewing people, staying up late, getting up early, eating lots of falafel and shawarma, and drinking tons of tea and coffee.

Of course, Chris and I thought it was amazing—which is what you think when you're the parent. But one day Anna called and asked if she could borrow thirty dollars to enter the film into the National Youth Film Festival. I didn't really know what that meant, but I said sure.

There were 250 documentaries entered, and theirs won Best Documentary that year. Hmmm. I guess it actually *was* good.

So here's the deal. In a few pages of this book, I just told you a story that consumed our family for two years. It cost us a bunch of money, took a gazillion hours of Anna's time—while she was in college—and caused not a little stress here and there. There were multiple times that she (and we) wanted to quit, or at least "put it on the back burner for now." Which, of course, is a euphemism for quitting. But she didn't.

Was the process scary? For sure. New things are always scary. They're always hard. Usually the reason something hasn't been done before, or at least that *you* haven't done it before, is that it's hard. And hard things make us worry.

Being scared, nervous, worried, or fearful is never really the issue. The real issue is what we do with those very natural emotions. Do they control us? Stop us? Or do we push through them and continue to say yes to the adventure Jesus calls us on?

Anna did. You should, too.

You Can Say No
If You Want To

> Never be afraid to trust an unknown future to a known God.
>
> Corrie ten Boom

> My sheep listen to my voice; I know them, and they follow me.
>
> Jesus

Much of what Chris and I have written so far is about saying yes to Jesus—thus, the title of the book. But what if you decide to say no? Well, as I enjoy doing, let me surprise you by saying that's okay. It's okay if you say no to Jesus.

Here's the thing: we aren't always 100 percent sure that an idea or opportunity or whatever is in front of us is from Jesus, right? If he was literally standing in front of you, clearly calling you, you'd go, right? Wrong. Let's think about this . . .

Consider following God in the Old Testament. The ones who did say yes made it into the "Hall of Faith" of Hebrews 11. That's why Abraham was such a big deal—he kept saying yes when God called. It wasn't 100 percent of the time, but he was better than most.

But what about our other heroes—like Moses? How'd he do? Not that well. He ran from God for forty years. That doesn't seem good.

How about our favorite man-after-God's-own-heart, David? I can't even start with him. Or Jonah. God called him to go to northern Iraq, but instead, he decided to take a ship in the opposite direction. Fishy.

Many of Israel's kings specifically decided not to follow God's way. Even prophets would come and remind them, and they still wouldn't go.

The children of Israel had the physical presence of God leading them by fire and cloud, and they mostly complained day and night. Then God rained food down on their heads, and what did they do? Yep, they complained.

Hop over with me to the New Testament for a minute. You'd think if you had the physical Jesus of Nazareth with you doing daily miracles, multiplying fish and bread, raising the dead, kicking out demons, and all that stuff, well, you'd do whatever he said, right?

But most people did not follow him. Oh, there were the bystanders. The crowds kept their distance and loved him for what he did and some of what he said. They loved that he gave the annoying religious leaders a hard time, but he seemed a bit soft on those mean, cruel Romans, saying things like "love your enemies" and "carry his pack two miles, not just one." And most didn't give up everything and follow him.

Even the Twelve seemed confused most of their time with Jesus. Peter's classic "Never, Lord!" statement (Matthew 16:22) got him a good rebuke, but he valiantly crashed ahead and told Jesus he would never leave or deny him. Peter was Jesus' number-one fan, he said. A few days later, he acted as if he'd never even heard of Jesus, let alone followed him for three years.

Before we come down hard on Peter, we should recognize that we say no to Jesus all the time, no matter how clear his calling is. Recently I have clearly felt God's Spirit nudge me to do or say something, but I haven't done it. I didn't kneel down, close my eyes, bow my head, and say, "Dear Jesus, no, I will not do that." I just didn't do it.

The only reason I say no—or do nothing—is because of fear. Sure, it might go by some of its pseudonyms: worry, concern, embarrassment, insecurity, pride, wisdom, or responsibility. But deep down, we only say no to Jesus' call out of some type of fear. Think about that for a bit.

I'm far from perfect, and I do tell God no sometimes. But every time I say yes, something good happens. Can we say no? Of course. And then that wonderful grace thing kicks in. God loves you exactly the same amount as he did before you said no. His love remains the same.

What *does* change is your ability to hear his voice. I find that when I've said no enough times in a certain area of my life, it becomes easier and easier to say no. After a while, we can't hear that still, small voice anymore. It just seems normal not to do what we've not been doing.

Consider our money. We all know that everything is God's— 100 percent of all we own is not actually ours; we're simply taking care of it. God loans it to us so we can use it to help others. That's it. That's the whole reason we make $20,000 a year or $2,000,000 a year. It's all God's, and he wants to use it—through us—to help others.

Then we have this funny thing called a tithe. It just means a "tenth." Of the 100 percent that we steward of God's, 10 percent is his in a unique way. It's holy. Set aside. Sanctified. Whatever term you want to use—it's his, sort of by definition. The other 90 percent we seem to have semiownership over, but not the 10 percent.

I love it when I hear good churchgoing Christians discuss

tithing. More and more I hear statements like "Well, you know, tithing is an Old Testament concept. Really, God wants it all. So I give it ALL to him." *Yeah, really? Who are you fooling?*

Growing up, the only conversations I heard were whether the 10 percent was off our gross or net income. I don't remember anyone asking whether it was biblical. I always figure we ought to err on the side of generosity. What, are we trying to sneak one over on God by giving 10 percent of our net income? Or trying to convince ourselves that because it's "all God's," we don't actually need to physically give 10 percent? If it's really all God's—which, of course, it is—then go ahead and give it all away—100 percent. Man, I think 10 percent of my gross income is a great deal from a generous God. Anyway, it's not about "deals"; it's about our saying yes. Why would we ever say no?

I think there are tons of things like that in the Scriptures—things that are crystal clear—yet we still say no.

Then there's that not-so-obvious still, small voice. What about that? How do you know if that voice is God's?

For a reprieve from all things Middle East, here are a couple of Stateside stories about hearing God's voice, showing that saying yes doesn't necessarily lead you far beyond your front door.

Years ago in our little church in Colorado Springs, there was this guy named Dave. Dave was awesome. He'd just been set free from some hard-core drugs and was still working on his drinking and pot smoking. But boy, did he ever love God. He was so so thankful for all God had done for him. Dave came to the weekly home group Chris and I led. Mostly a bunch of messed-up people being led by us, who didn't know anything.

Our group had been going through the book of Acts and talking about how God still wants to speak to us—that all we have to do is listen, and then do what he says.

One Sunday at church, after the service, we had some extra time to pray for folks who wanted it. It was one of those special God moments. I was just standing there sort of observing, probably acting like I was intently listening to God, but most likely thinking about getting pizza at Old Chicago afterward with some friends. Anyway, Dave came beside me and tapped me on the shoulder. "Hey, Carl, I think I might have heard God say something to me."

"Wow, Dave, that's awesome. What was it?"

"Well, I'm not sure it's God, but I just sort of had this idea to go over and tell that new guy that God loves him." And then Dave started almost crying, he was so scared. "So what do you think?" he asked.

"Dave, my guess is that God does, in fact, love that guy, and I think it'd be amazing if you went over there and told him that." The next thing I knew, Dave was hugging that guy and they were both crying. I never knew the rest of the story, but I'm pretty sure Dave heard from God that day.

I remember one time when Chris and I were having breakfast at our favorite little restaurant in the mountains here in Colorado. Just the two of us. It was a big splurge for us to go out those days. We were tight financially. But as we ate, we both kept getting drawn to this family of five sitting across the room. All of a sudden Chris blurted out to me, "I think we should buy their breakfast." I immediately knew that was right. I don't know how she "knew," and I'm not sure how I "knew," but we both knew.

So we got the waitress's attention and told her to put the family's check on ours and we'd pay for both. We meant it to be a secret, but the family found out, and the mom and dad came over to our table to thank us. They ended up asking us why we wanted to pay their bill. Chris and I both said something like, "As weird as this might sound, we think God told us to."

The wife started to cry and the man slumped down in the chair beside us. They begin to tell us their story. How they had just moved there and didn't know anyone. That they were Christians, but had started to wonder about God and whether he even cared for them. The man said something I'll never forget: "Today we were just taking the kids and driving up the mountain. I'd told God this morning that if something didn't happen today, well, I don't know, but—" His voice trailed off and he teared up.

After a moment, he continued, "Today God has spoken. He is real, and I know he does care. Thank you!"

We heard. We said a very simple yes. It cost us about thirty bucks, and it may have saved a life. At the least, it set a whole family on a path back toward God. We never saw them again.

Here are a couple of good principles to remember when it comes to hearing God's voice:

1. If it's counterintuitive, it just might be God. I half-jokingly tell people that I wake up each day, think about what I want to do, and then try to do the opposite.

2. If it's positive, go ahead and do it. Telling someone God loves them is always a good idea, 100 percent of the time. Buying a stranger lunch is always a good idea. Never a bad one. Do it. Mowing the neighbor's yard. Go ahead. Saying a kind word at the mailbox. Praying for someone who is sick. Go ahead. No need to wait. In fact, I'm guessing that God is telling you to do that.

3. If you think it might be God, and it doesn't hurt anyone, and it might help them, take a risk. Inviting your neighbor to church—can't hurt. Taking your family on that mission trip to Africa—might cost you a lot, but it's got to be good. Go for it.

Now, here are some examples of when you need to be skeptical of the "still, small voice." If you have an issue with drinking and you think God wants you to start a bar ministry—not God.

If it can potentially hurt your spouse or kids (even just being gone too much), then at the very least, you should talk it through with them first.

If it costs you money you literally don't have, then be careful; get counsel. I'm not a believer of putting a mission trip on a credit card you can't pay off. If God wants you to go, he'll find a way to pay for it without your going in to debt.

The wisdom of God often looks like foolishness to man, but there is wisdom from God that's also just plain normal, when you are walking with him. Not going into debt is wise—so is caring for your family and not stepping into places that will play to your weaknesses. Be wise in God's wisdom.

You can say no to Jesus, but if you do it too much you'll stop hearing his voice.

Are there things in your life that you've been ignoring God's voice about for so long that they just seem normal? If you're quiet for a minute, you'll know what you're doing is not right. Are there temptations you've given in to so often that they've become a justifiable part of your life? Do you work sixty hours or more a week and say things like, "It's for my family," or "It's just for a season." Don't fool yourself.

If you've been saying (or doing) *no* so long it seems okay, well, be honest and reassess the situation. Ask for some help.

Come on—be real here. Let your spouse or someone you know and trust speak the truth to you. Ask them, "Are there things that you see in me that are clearly not pleasing to God? I want to be a person who says yes to Jesus when he calls—not no. Can you help me?" If all else fails, ask your kids. They'll tell you the truth.

That's some gutsy living right there. Not many people will do it. You might read past all this and keep going. And it's okay. Honestly, I'm not being facetious. It's really all right. God will love and accept you just as you are. No strings attached. And he'll even keep inviting you to say yes. He won't give up on you. Isn't that the coolest thing ever? God doesn't give up on us.

If you keep saying no, though, you are choosing to take yourself out of the adventure. You'll begin *not* to hear his voice. You won't get to see the family's teary eyes when they thank you, or the Daves of the world hugging the stranger, or your neighbors coming to know Jesus and turning their lives around because you jumped in with both feet. So why would you not want to say yes?

But again, you can say no . . .

17

Courage Lost

They were on their way up to Jerusalem, with Jesus leading the way, and the disciples were astonished, while those who followed were afraid. Again he took the Twelve aside and told them what was going to happen to him.

Mark 10:32

I learned that courage was not the absence of fear, but the triumph over it. The brave man is not he who does not feel afraid, but he who conquers that fear.

Nelson Mandela

. . . but just in case you *do* want to live a life of saying yes to Jesus, here's where it could take you.

Fear. You will be afraid. Yep, I know that sounds like the opposite of what I've been saying, but if you think that, then you haven't been reading carefully. You will be afraid, for sure. You will fail. And you'll die. I think I mentioned the dying part already, but just in case you missed that—good news—you're gonna die. And you won't know when. I don't. I could die later today (I just hope I can at least finish this book first). Or it could be in forty years. None of us knows. Sounds a little freaky, doesn't it? Most people don't say it so bluntly, but I'm trying to help you to be honest and expose your deepest fears. You can't deal with them if you don't know what they are.

Thanks to Paul, we know that "to die is gain" (Philippians 1:21). He even pokes fun at death by saying, "Where, O death, is your sting?" (1 Corinthians 15:55). So know there's nothing to fear. In fact, it may be something to anticipate.

Yeah, yeah, but we do fear death. And we are afraid to fail and look stupid and that our kids won't turn out well and . . . mostly we are not people of great bravery and courage. We go along with the crowd; we aren't the ones who forge a new path and stand against the tide. If we ever had courage in the first place, we seem to lose it daily. And I'm the same. I'm chicken-hearted. Don't believe me? Let me tell you a few more stories.

First of all, growing up, I was little. I mean, like, short. Small. I wrestled in the ninety-six-pound weight class as a freshman in high school (fourteen years old). And I was bad. Mostly got pinned in the first round.

I was geeky—a nerd. I didn't have many friends, and the ones I did have didn't have other friends. I wasn't a jock or a scholar. Wasn't in the bad kids group either—I wasn't strong enough to be one of them. I was kind of nothing. Always had just one or two friends, never more. I was afraid of not being liked, which is weird, since I wasn't liked. I got beat up after school a lot. When I wasn't getting beat up, I was being chased home by the bullies who wanted to beat me up. But since I wasn't very fast, they usually caught me—and beat me up. There were no anti-bullying campaigns in the late sixties and early seventies, but if there were, I'd have been their poster child.

I didn't have confidence—didn't think I would be anybody. I was afraid of my own shadow. I don't really know why I was that way, either. I suppose some percentage was my parents' fault. Some was my environment. Some was just me and my responses. I don't know. It's in the past. I've gotten over it. I love my parents and we have a great relationship, and I've learned to see the good from my childhood.

I just want you to know that I wasn't born with some kind of *Braveheart* spirit that gave me a head start at being a courageous, perfect follower of Jesus. Not at all. I was born a coward, which was confirmed most of my life. In fact, I felt like a loser.

Fast-forward to my life as a forty-year-old missionary to Beirut. I was no longer a coward. I was "Carl of Beirut." Minister to the baddest of the bad. The tough crowd. The Hezbollah. Political leaders. I knew the Scriptures through and through, and few could out-argue me in the areas of missions, evangelism, church planting, and generally everything "Jesus." I hadn't written my first book yet, but I held conferences that people flew in for from around the world. I was an expert (which it says on the backs of my books—which makes it official).

Except much of what was driving me was proving to myself and the world that I was *not* a loser. I was not afraid. And I'd work till I proved them all wrong for thinking I was.

So instead of being a "loser," I became driven. I worked harder than anyone else. I said yes to everything that was in front of me. Not the yes I'm talking about in this book, but a simpleminded, non-Jesus yes. A yes born from insecurity and a sense of low (or no) self-worth. Not a yes birthed out of a heart of love for and gratitude to my heavenly Father because he loved me so much, but the dutiful yes of a slave. Of the older son.

Enter my dear friend Floyd McClung. He was visiting us in Beirut, and after one long evening of his talking to Chris and me about our marriage and my over-busy life, he looked at me and said, "Carl, you need to go to Healing for the Nations in Georgia—you're messed up, dude."

What? First of all, what about Chris? Isn't she messed up? And Georgia? We're in Beirut. And . . . it's expensive. And it's a week long; I don't have that kind of time—I'm busy saving the Middle East. And, well, I don't want to sit around with a bunch of screwed-up people sharing my issues and crying. That's just not me! I'm way too cool for that school.

I said no to Floyd.

Three months later, I was in Georgia.

You can check out the ministry called Healing for the Nations yourself—just Google it (they're now based near Kansas City). They typically have ten to twelve leader types attend each session for a variety of reasons, such as needing to reconnect with God or because of broken relationships, etc. But my time there consisted of two older divorced women and me. I was somewhat offended. Actually, angry that I seemed to be wasting a week of my time.

Day 1 was a bunch of teaching about how much God loves us and all that jazz. *I know that, thanks anyway. How much does this cost?* Then we were assigned some long quiet times to walk in the woods with a little homework. I can't tell you how indignant I was about being there.

This nice couple, Steve and Rujon, led the meetings with their helper, Marie, an intern. I could tell they all meant well and were trying their best, so I decided I should at least be nice and pay attention—that was Day 2.

They spent some significant time on 2 Corinthians 10:3–5:

> For though we live in the world, we do not wage war as the world does. The weapons we fight with are not the weapons of the world. On the contrary, they have divine power to demolish strongholds. We demolish arguments and every pretension

that sets itself up against the knowledge of God, and we take captive every thought to make it obedient to Christ.

As of Day 2, I was figuring out the bottom-line lesson (which I was good at doing; that way I could sleep through the rest of the time). Here it is, in simple bullet points:

- We have believed things that are not true as if they were true.
- We believe things about ourselves and about God that are not true.
- Out of these (wrong) beliefs, we live our lives.
- We have to recognize what those wrong beliefs are and identify them.
- Once we've done that, we can demolish these strongholds (a "stronghold" being one of these false beliefs).

Okay. I got it. It was fairly straightforward. So now I needed to figure out what my strongholds were. The leaders, whom I liked a little better now than on Day 1—but not by much—told us that we would each meet with a member of their team and try to discern the stronghold or strongholds in our lives. We would know something was a stronghold when it involved an "I am" statement, like "I am no good," or "I am not loved." To say "I am" was to make it personal and to expose that we actually do believe this is who we are—our actual identity. And then we'd name it, expose it to the light, pray about it, see what God said about that thing (truth), and we'd be free. *Voila!*

Okay, I was ready. *Let's git-r-done!*

Of course, I didn't even get one of the main leaders; I got the intern, Marie. *Figures*, I thought. *The two really messed-up*

186

women must need the big dogs more than me, so I guess it's okay.

We'd been given a worksheet to help us identify our strongholds—our bad beliefs—and I'd done mine, but it hadn't really worked. So when Marie and I sat down at the picnic table outside the lodge where we were meeting and she asked if I "had anything," I just said nope, with sort of a finality. Basically, I was saying, "I'm fine."

She asked a few questions. You know the type—annoying, deeply perceptive questions. The kind that make you think, *Wow, why'd you ask that?*

As I started to be a bit more honest about my childhood and how I used to feel like a loser, she asked me the obvious—if that was a stronghold. "Are you a loser? Do you feel like one?"

I remember saying something along the lines of "Huh, me? A loser? I don't think so. Ask anyone who knows me. No way."

"I didn't ask what others think of you," she said. "I asked what you feel about yourself."

Okay, now she was getting all psychological on me. You know that counselor stuff, where you need to lie down on a couch. That just wasn't me. I wasn't afraid or anything; I just didn't want to go there.

After another fifteen minutes of questions I didn't want to answer, Marie said, "How about we do this? You just try saying the words *I'm a loser* and see what happens."

I may have replied, "Well, I would if it was true, but it's not true, since I'm quite obviously not a loser. I mean, maybe I was once, but now I'm quite a successful leader."

Marie kept pushing me to say those words. Of course, the more she pushed, the more I resisted. *What kind of psychobabble is this?*

"Saying the words doesn't do anything," I told her.

"Well, you may be right," she said. "So if they don't matter, just go ahead and try saying the words *I am a loser* and see how it feels."

Ugh. I hate that word feels. *Who cares how it feels? I am about to feel my way right on out of here in about five minutes. That'll show them what it feels like.*

Fortunately (in this case), I was as afraid of looking mean as I was of my feelings, so I agreed to say the words.

"I am a . . ."

I couldn't do it.

I told her I shouldn't lie, so I didn't want to say something that wasn't true. I told her I shouldn't say things that bring up the distant past. I told her other stuff I can't remember now because it's all sort of a blur. She just smiled and nodded.

I tried one more time—I decided to just force it. *Who cares if I mean it or if it is true—I'll just say the stupid words.*

"I am a loser," I blurted out.

When the *rrrr* sound at the end of the word *loser* left my lips, something happened. I think an alien took over my body, because I started crying so hard that I hit my head on the wooden picnic table. Not sure how that happened. I only remember my head being stuck to the table and snot and tears and loud noises coming out of my mouth. After about five minutes, Marie kindly handed me a box of Kleenex and told me that I had a red smudge of color on my nose from the table. I wiped and blew and cried some more, and all the while she just sat there with a kind but knowing and understanding look on her face, as if to say, "It's okay, honey. I've seen this many times; it's not a biggie."

"Well, well," I said after recovering enough to speak. "I guess this must mean something." (I'm so perceptive.)

There's obviously much more to this story—God really has been setting me free from being so driven. I've experienced significant freedom from my fear of being a nobody—of being a loser like I was when I was a kid. I'm not totally out of the woods. I still deal with the fear of people not liking or respecting me. I often think no one will listen and no one cares what I think or say because, why would they?

Writing this (or any) book is torture, to say the least. I have fear every night that it's not going to make any sense, and if it does somehow make sense, no one will want to read it, and if someone does accidentally end up reading it, they won't like it—and thus they won't like me and that's because I'm a loser anyway. And who likes losers?

But mostly, I know that's not true. God likes me. I have a great set of friends and a wonderful family who like me. And I get lots of nice messages and emails from people who say that something I wrote or said or did helped them in some way.

But still, nothing makes me more insecure than writing down my thoughts for the whole world to read—and critique. And yet, here I am, writing this book on fear.

That's it. I am afraid. I am a chickenhearted, earthbound human being just like you. Full of questions and insecurities about who I am and why I matter and what you'll think of the things I produce. Not that different from my children when they'd bring home their latest school project and show it to Chris and me, just hoping we'd approve. In the end, maybe we're all just kids.

And maybe that's what God wants. To enter his kingdom, we must become like children, Jesus said. What if God knows we're all afraid, and he's okay with it? He just wants us to come to him with our fears and insecurities and get the needed affirmation there. At his feet, rather than from the false and fleeting affirmations of the world. Maybe at the feet of the Father is where we can find courage again.

Courage Found

You gain strength, courage, and confidence by every experience in which you really stop to look fear in the face. You are able to say to yourself, "I lived through this horror. I can take the next thing that comes along."

Eleanor Roosevelt

Next to him was Eleazar son of Dodai the Ahohite, one of the three mighty warriors. He was with David at Pas Dammim when the Philistines gathered there for battle. At a place where there was a field full of barley, the troops fled from the Philistines. But they took their stand in the middle of the field. They defended it and struck the Philistines down, and the Lord brought about a great victory.

1 Chronicles 11:12–14

Chris

Reminiscing about our early days in Lebanon makes me realize that Carl really operated out of the belief that "I can do all things through Christ who strengthens me." He was always willing to try new things and didn't let fear hold him back. Usually when he told me about an idea, I would start to bite my nails, unsure how things would turn out. For instance, that time he preached in a big tent in the south of Lebanon made me a bit nervous. But my trust in God was desperately deepened and my faith was stretched beyond confined borders. As I released Carl to be obedient to what God called him to do, I realized that some people were hearing the good news for the first time. I will say that after he preached there, our family felt increased pressure for a while. He was asked to not go back and received an anonymous death threat. We were also asked by our own government to leave the country, but before we were to leave there was a small window of time, and Carl was asked to speak about Jesus in the south again. The stakes now seemed higher, so when Carl asked if I thought he should take the trip, my immediate response was no.

"Did you pray about it?" he asked.

I told him I was so busy watching our kids that I never had a chance. So he played with the kids while I went to a quiet place and prayed. After a few minutes I heard God say to me, "You need to offer up Carl just as Abraham offered up Isaac." I went and told Carl, and we both agreed he should go to share the good news again before we would have to leave Lebanon. I had a peace that truly passed all understanding. Carl went back down and shared God's love, and many people were encouraged and blessed—and my hubby returned home safely. Whew! Again my heart was encouraged by God's amazing love.

Remember back in chapter 3 when I told you the story of how God healed the man's leg in Cana? Well, the news spread, as you might expect. In fact, the tent became called the Tent of Healing, which is sort of funny since no one (that I know of) got healed in the tent. I liked it, but it did add a bit of pressure. The Tent of Healing sounded more like an Oral Roberts or

Benny Hinn campaign than a few knuckleheads like us who had no idea what we were doing.

Several days after the healing, we set up the tent in a different town in the south of Lebanon. People in two different towns had been vying for us to come to their town. But the second day in the new town we chose, about twenty miles inland from Tyre, was rainy. Like, very very rainy. Like, shut-the-meeting-down-'cause-it's-raining-so-hard-we-can't-get-to-the-tent rainy. My friend Fouad and I were standing outside the tent, in a mud-up-to-your-ankle field, and I felt discouraged. Over-the-top bummed out. The night before had been a huge success with people coming from all over the south, and more were promised for tonight. But it was going to be impossible.

As Fouad and I stood there, not sure if the water running down our cheeks was rain or tears, I looked across the street and noticed the local mosque. Somehow I'd missed that before. We'd set up the tent in the public square, but I hadn't noticed that we were across the street from a mosque. I opened my mouth.

"Fouad—" I started to say.

He quickly interrupted me. "Carl, Carl—I know what you're thinking, and no. No, we cannot meet in the mosque."

"Wow, how did you know that's what I was thinking?"

"I know you're just crazy enough to have such a dumb thought," Fouad replied with a smile on his face but concern in his voice.

"Yeah, but I just wonder if we could? I mean, has anyone ever tried?"

"No, because you can't."

But I've run into that response most of my life. The ol' you-can't-do-that-because-no-one's-ever-done-it-before answer. It's really sort of a dumb point, if you think about it, right? By definition, no one has ever done anything before it was first done.

I convinced Fouad we should at least try. As a foreigner, I'd play on their sense of wonderful Arab hospitality and see if that'd work. We walked across the street to the mosque. It was locked and no one was there. Someone saw us from across the street and came over to ask if we needed something. I said that we wanted to talk to the imam. And this nice man took us down the street about four blocks to his home.

We knocked on the door and the imam answered. This was actually a little more awkward than I'd thought it would be. "Ummm, my name is Carl, and we're doing that tent thing down the street, and—"

"I know who you are. Come in."

We backed away at first. I'm such a Westerner—always in a hurry to get to the point and forgetting that we should sit, be polite, talk about our families and the weather, then have some tea and cookies, and then, only then, bring up why we were there. *I should know better by now*, I thought to myself as we went inside.

After perhaps fifteen minutes, I knew it was okay to ask my question. "Sir," I began, "we are here in your city with this tent, speaking to people about how wonderful Jesus is, and as you can see outside, it's raining. And the field where our tent is pitched, right across the street from your mosque, is too muddy to get to. And we, I mean I, was wondering if it'd be possible to use your mosque tonight for our gathering. I've heard that folks are coming from all around to your town tonight, and it'd be a shame to have to turn them away. What do you think? I know this is an unusual request, but—"

"That's fine."

"Excuse me?" I replied, a bit stunned.

"Yes, I think that's fine, but it's really not in my jurisdiction to make that call. You'll have to ask the local Hezbollah leader for his permission."

My excitement was short-lived. I think it was Fouad who asked the obvious but slightly offensive question, "So you don't have the authority to let us use your mosque?" I do remember wondering if a Muslim group came to my church here in the United States and said they were having some meetings about how wonderful the prophet Muhammad was and asked if they could use our church building tonight, what our pastor's response might be. I'm sure it'd be something like "Let me check with the elder board and get back with you about that."

So we found ourselves walking back down the same street, past the mosque and the tent, to the house of the local Hezbollah guy. I wasn't quitting just yet. We knocked—he answered. By the way, these guys were home because it was about two in the afternoon—lunchtime.

"Come in and have some lunch with us," was his answer to our knock. He didn't know us—didn't know who we were or why we were there. I'm always stunned by that. Do I do that when two strange men knock at my door during mealtime? (That's a rhetorical question, of course. It doesn't actually need to be answered for us to continue this story.)

We sat down. We ate. We chatted. I remembered my Middle Eastern manners this time. No quickly diving in to the issue at house number two. After half an hour or more, I asked my question. Told him about the meeting with the imam up the street. Explained the tent and why we were doing what we were doing and that we needed his permission to use the mosque.

"Well, that's up to the imam," he replied with feigned consternation on his face. "Sorry."

Again, I may not be the sharpest tool in the shed, but I'm not totally dumb. Neither one wanted the responsibility of saying yes, so they were passing it off to the other. I've played that game. And I know how to win it.

"Well, if the imam said it was okay, would you say it was okay?"

"Sure," he proclaimed with some confidence.

"Perfect," I replied with a smile, "because he said it was okay as long as you said it was okay."

"Really? Well, then it's fine with me."

We marched back up the road to the imam's house with a serious bounce to our steps—dancing in the rain, maybe—and told the imam the good news. He just said, "Really? Wow. Okay, then, here are the keys." He handed them to us, told us where the lights were and where the power generator was in case the electricity went out, and said, "*Ahlan wa Sahlan*" (Welcome to my mosque).

We had the meeting there that night and it was packed. Went great. First time preaching in a mosque for me. And it wouldn't be the last.

Postscript

'm done writing the book. This thing freaked me out like nothing I've done before—not sure why. It's taken me two years of stopping and starting. Writing and rewriting. Trashing whole chapters and sections only to wish I had them back. Sleepless nights. Confusion. Fear.

In writing this book about the adventure of following Jesus and saying yes to him, I've come face-to-face with my own insecurities, weaknesses, and fears in a whole new way. I think I've decided my number-one fear is fear. Fear scares me to death. I don't like it, don't want it, preach against it—and I have it. I guess FDR was right when he said, "The only thing we have to fear is fear itself."

And here's the last one—the one I want you to walk away with if you forget everything else in this book (which you will). It's the central thesis of this book, and I was reminded to restate it while talking to a close friend as I finished writing. He sort of knew that I'd be writing a book on fear, or faith, or saying yes, or . . . as he said it, "probably something about Jesus." I told him he was correct on all fronts.

"But what's the bottom-line point?" he asked. I think he was trying to get out of reading the book, so he wanted the shortest possible CliffsNotes version. It made me think.

"It's a book about overcoming our fears. We have them, but we're called to follow Jesus in and through them. And when we do that, we are led into an incredible lifelong adventure. Too many of us are bound by fear that cripples us. We're convinced the Muslims are coming. The [fill in the blank] are taking over, and the economy is collapsing—"

"Yeah, but," he interrupted, "how do we know if it's fear, or if we really do need to stand against these things and fight for what's right?"

Now *that's* the question! And I think I actually know the answer.

The opposite of fear is love. It's not bravery or courage. It's love. Love casts out fear. So you either love or fear something or someone. Love motivates you to appropriate action; fear binds you and causes you to freeze in place. In the end, the adventure of saying yes to Jesus is a journey of love conquering fear. That's it. Every day we have to make that choice perhaps dozens of times. Love—don't fear.

I will close with the prayer of one of my all-time favorite people—a man who said yes to Jesus over and over: the apostle Paul. Let his prayer for the Ephesians be ours as well.

> I pray that you, being rooted and established in love, may have power, together with all the Lord's holy people, to grasp how wide and long and high and deep is the love of Christ, and to know this love that surpasses knowledge—that you may be

filled to the measure of all the fullness of God. Now to him who is able to do immeasurably more than all we ask or imagine, according to his power that is at work within us.

And we say yes.

Acknowledgments

Writing a book is never a solo enterprise. This one, especially. Chris and our three young-adult children have all contributed. It is our story. Our family, plus a lot of God and a gazillion friends—friends in the Middle East and others here in the West who have shaped how we think, how we live, and the words on these pages. You know who you are.

Andy and Jeff at Bethany House are so fun to work with. This is our second project together, and it's been a joy. They are personal, professional, and they "get" what I'm writing about.

Thank you to Jan for your help, as well as to Jay and Jesse, who were my first readers. They persevered through a messy early manuscript and gave great input. Then our dear friend June took it and spent dozens of hours with me working through the book two times. Thank you all for your hard work.

Carl Medearis is an international expert in the field of Arab-American and Muslim-Christian relations.

He acts as a catalyst for a number of current movements in the Middle East to promote peacemaking as well as cultural, political, and religious dialogue leading toward reconciliation. He is the author of the acclaimed book on these issues *Muslims, Christians, and Jesus*, as well as *Speaking of Jesus* and *Tea with Hezbollah* (coauthored with Ted Dekker).

Carl, his wife, Chris, and three kids lived in Beirut, Lebanon, for twelve years. Through their unique and strategic approach around the Arab world, they encouraged university students, business professionals, and political leaders to live their lives by the principles and teachings of Jesus in order to change their societies and nations.

Today Carl spends much of his time working with leaders both in the West and in the Arab world with the hope of seeing the Arab Middle East and the West experience full and fruitful relationships through the life and teachings of Jesus of Nazareth. Learn more at www.carlmedearis.com.

More From Carl Medearis

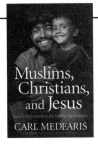

In this book, Medearis provides new insights into the top questions people have about Muslims, Muhammad, and Islam. With practical information and fascinating stories, he shares culturally sensitive ways for Christians to get to know Muslims on a personal level. You will learn:

- How Islam's "Pillars of Faith" are lived out in today's world
- What the Qur'an says about women
- What Muslims think about the Bible and Jesus
- How to bring up spiritual matters in conversations
- And much more

Rather than initially focusing on the differences between Islam and Christianity, Medearis shows how common ground is the best foundation for friendships and for hearts turning to Jesus.

Named an *Outreach* Magazine Resource of the Year

Muslims, Christians, and Jesus
by Carl Medearis